—◊◊—

God's Answers
for Your
Every Question
for Mothers

—◊◊—

**ALBURY
PUBLISHING**
TULSA, OKLAHOMA

2nd Printing

God's Answers for Your Every Question for Mothers

ISBN 1-57778-047-7
Copyright © 1998 by ALBURY PUBLISHING
P.O. Box 470406
Tulsa, Oklahoma 74147-0406

CONTENTS

LORD, PLEASE HELP ME
PARENT MY CHILD

TABLE OF CONTENTS

BEING A MOTHER ISN'T EASY—
I NEED YOUR COMFORT, LORD

THE BASIS OF IT ALL—
A RELATIONSHIP WITH GOD

---◈◈◈---

Q: So much has changed since the Bible was written. How can I be sure its answers still apply to my life today?

---◈◈◈---

A: Even if it was written in Scripture long ago, you can be sure it's written for us.

ROMANS 15:4 THE MESSAGE

Every Scripture is God-breathed — given by His inspiration.

2 TIMOTHY 3:16 AMP

"I tell you the truth, until heaven and earth disappear, not the smallest letter, not the least stroke of a pen, will by any means disappear from the Law until everything is accomplished."

MATTHEW 5:18 NIV

"People are like grass that dies away; their beauty fades as quickly as the beauty of wildflowers. The grass withers, and the flowers fall away. But the word of the Lord will last forever."

1 PETER 1:24,25 NLT

Every part of Scripture is...useful one way or another — showing us truth, exposing our rebellion, correcting our mistakes, training us to live God's way.

2 TIMOTHY 3:16 THE MESSAGE

The word of God is living and powerful.

HEBREWS 4:12 NKJV

They are not just idle words for you — they are your life.

DEUTERONOMY 32:47 NIV

PRAYERS

Open my eyes to see the wonderful truths in your law.

PSALM 119:18 NLT

Forever, O Lord, your word stands firm in heaven. Your faithfulness extends to every generation, as enduring as the earth you created. Your laws remain true today, for everything serves your plans.

PSALM 119:89-91 NLT

From studying your laws, I found out long ago that you made them to last forever. All you say can be trusted; your teachings are true and will last forever.

PSALM 119:152,160 CEV

PROMISES

The law of the Lord is perfect, reviving the soul. The decrees of the Lord are trustworthy, making wise the simple. The commandments of the Lord are right, bringing joy to the heart. The commands of the Lord are clear, giving insight to life.

The laws of the Lord are true; each one is fair. They are more desirable than gold, even the finest gold. They are sweeter than honey, even honey dripping from the comb. They are a warning to those who hear them; there is great reward for those who obey them.

PSALM 19:7-11 NLT

"Heaven and earth will pass away, but My words will not pass away."

MATTHEW 24:35 NASB

Q: GOD, YOU'RE THE ULTIMATE FATHER. HOW DO YOU TREAT YOUR CHILDREN?

A: He surrounds me with lovingkindness and tender mercies. He fills my life with good things!

PSALM 103:4,5 TLB

The Lord is merciful and gracious; he is slow to get angry and full of unfailing love. He will not constantly accuse us, nor remain angry forever. He has not punished us for all our sins, nor does he deal with us as we deserve. For his unfailing love toward those who fear him is as great as the height of the heavens above the earth. He has removed our rebellious acts as far away from us as the east is from the west.

The Lord is like a father to his children, tender and compassionate to those who fear him. For he understands how weak we are; he knows we are only dust.

PSALM 103:8-14 NLT

Whatever is good and perfect comes to us
from God above, who created all heaven's
lights. Unlike them, he never changes or casts
shifting shadows. In his goodness he chose to
make us his own children by giving us his true
word. And we, out of all creation, became his
choice possession.

JAMES 1:17,18 NLT

If God gives such attention to the appearance
of wildflowers — most of which are never even
seen — don't you think he'll attend to you,
take pride in you, do his best for you?

MATTHEW 6:30 THE MESSAGE

I will instruct you and teach you in the way
which you should go; I will counsel you with
My eye upon you.

PSALM 32:8 NASB

Your ears shall hear a word behind you, saying, "This is the way, walk in it," whenever
you turn to the right hand or whenever you
turn to the left.

ISAIAH 30:21 NKJV

"The Lord corrects the people he loves and
disciplines those he calls his own."

HEBREWS 12:6 CEV

The Father is a merciful God, who always gives us comfort. He comforts us when we are in trouble, so that we can share that same comfort with others in trouble.

2 CORINTHIANS 1:3,4 CEV

And we have known and believed the love that God has for us. God is love. We love Him because He first loved us.

1 JOHN 4:16,19 NKJV

We used to be stupid, disobedient, and foolish, as well as slaves of all sorts of desires and pleasures. We were evil and jealous. Everyone hated us, and we hated everyone. God our Savior showed us how good and kind he is. He saved us because of his mercy, and not because of any good things that we have done. God washed us by the power of the Holy Spirit. He gave us new birth and a fresh beginning. God sent Jesus Christ our Savior to give us his Spirit.

TITUS 3:3-6 CEV

It was all his doing; we had nothing to do with it. He gave us a good bath, and we came out of it new people, washed inside and out by the Holy Spirit.

TITUS 3:4-7 THE MESSAGE

PROMISES

"For the eyes of the Lord run to and fro throughout the whole earth, to show Himself strong on behalf of those whose heart is loyal to Him."

2 CHRONICLES 16:9 NKJV

He is a rewarder of those who diligently seek Him.

HEBREWS 11:6 NKJV

The Lord is faithful, and He will strengthen and protect you from the evil one.

2 THESSALONIANS 3:3 NASB

"As a mother comforts her child, so will I comfort you."

ISAIAH 66:13 NIV

And therefore the Lord [earnestly] waits — expectant, looking and longing — to be gracious to you, and therefore He lifts Himself up that He may have mercy on you and show loving-kindness to you...Blessed — happy, fortunate [to be envied] are all those who [earnestly] wait for Him, who expect and look and long for Him [for His victory, His favor, His love, His peace, His joy and His matchless, unbroken companionship].... He will surely be gracious to you at the sound of your cry; when He hears it, He will answer you.

ISAIAH 30:18,19 AMP

"Can a mother forget the baby at her breast and have no compassion on the child she has borne? Though she may forget, I will not forget you! See, I have engraved you on the palms of my hands."

ISAIAH 49:15,16 NIV

"They will be mine," says the Lord Almighty, "in the day when I make up my treasured possession. I will spare them, just as in compassion a man spares his son who serves him."

MALACHI 3:17 NIV

"The Lord your God in your midst, The Mighty One, will save; He will rejoice over you with gladness, He will quiet you with His love, He will rejoice over you with singing."

ZEPHANIAH 3:17 NKJV

The Lord is gracious and compassionate, slow to anger and rich in love. The Lord is good to all; he has compassion on all he has made.

PSALM 145:8,9 NIV

Q: GOD, WHAT KIND OF
MOTHER DO YOU WANT ME TO
BE? WHAT SHOULD I BE DOING
FOR MY KIDS?

A: Be imitators of God — copy Him and
follow His example — as well-beloved children
[imitate their father]. And walk in love —
esteeming and delighting in one another — as
Christ loved us and gave Himself up for us.

EPHESIANS 5:1,2 AMP

INSTRUCTIONS

Above all, love each other deeply, because love
covers over a multitude of sins.

1 PETER 4:8 NIV

Let love be your guide.

EPHESIANS 5:2 CEV

Put on a heart of compassion, kindness, humility, gentleness and patience; bearing with one

another, and forgiving each other, whoever has a complaint against anyone; just as the Lord forgave you, so also should you. Beyond all these things put on love, which is the perfect bond of unity.

COLOSSIANS 3:12-14 NASB

Carry each other's burdens, and in this way you will fulfill the law of Christ.

GALATIANS 6:2 NIV

Pray at all times — on every occasion, in every season — in the Spirit, with all [manner of] prayer and entreaty.

EPHESIANS 6:18 AMP

Let the word [spoken by] the Christ, the Messiah, have its home (in your hearts and minds) and dwell in you in [all its] richness, as you teach and admonish and train one another in all ght and intelligence and wisdom.

COLOSSIANS 3:16 AMP

Let the Word of Christ — the Message — have the run of the house. Give it plenty of room in your lives.... And sing, sing your hearts out to God! Let every detail in your lives — words, actions, whatever — be done in the name of the Master, Jesus, thanking God the Father every step of the way.

COLOSSIANS 3:16,17 THE MESSAGE

Correct your son, and he will give you comfort; he will also delight your soul.

PROVERBS 29:17 NASB

Train up a child in the way he should go, even when he is old he will not depart from it.

PROVERBS 22:6 NASB

Rear them [tenderly] in the training and discipline and the counsel and admonition of the Lord.

EPHESIANS 6:4 AMP

I will teach you hidden lessons from our past — stories we have heard and know, stories our ancestors handed down to us. We will not hide these truths from our children but will tell the next generation about the glorious deeds of the Lord. We will tell of his power and the mighty miracles he did...So each generation can set its hope anew on God, remembering his glorious miracles and obeying his commands.

PSALM 78:2-4,7 NLT

If someone is caught in a sin, you who are spiritual should restore him gently.

GALATIANS 6:1 NIV

Do not be bitter or angry or mad. Never shout angrily or say things to hurt others. Never do anything evil.

EPHESIANS 4:31 NCV

Do not provoke or irritate or fret your children — do not be hard on them or harass them; lest they become discouraged and sullen and morose and inferior and frustrated; do not break their spirit.

COLOSSIANS 3:21 AMP

Take them by the hand and lead them in the way of the Master.

EPHESIANS 6:4 THE MESSAGE

As a father loves and pities his children, so the Lord loves and pities those who fear Him — with reverence, worship and awe. For He knows our frame; He [earnestly] remembers and imprints [on his heart] that we are dust.

PSALM 103:13,14 AMP

Gently encourage the stragglers, and reach out for the exhausted, pulling them to their feet. Be patient with each person, attentive to individual needs.... Look for the best in each other, and always do your best to bring it out.

1 THESSALONIANS 5:14,15 THE MESSAGE

With each of you we were like a father with his child, holding your hand, whispering encouragement, showing you step by step how to live well before God, who called us into his own kingdom, into this delightful life.

1 THESSALONIANS 2:11,12 THE MESSAGE

We insisted that you live good lives for God, who calls you to his glorious kingdom.

1 THESSALONIANS 2:12 NCV

"As for me and my house, we will serve the Lord."

JOSHUA 24:15 NASB

PRAYER

May the God of peace...equip you with every-thing good for doing his will, and may he work in us what is pleasing to him, through Jesus Christ, to whom be glory for ever and ever. Amen.

HEBREWS 13:20,21 NIV

Q: WHAT IS GOD'S PURPOSE FOR MY FAMILY?

A: He seeks godly offspring.

MALACHI 2:15 NKJV

Now the Lord said to Abram, "Go forth from your country, and from your relatives and from your father's house, to the land which I will show you; and I will make you a great nation, and I will bless you.... And in you all the families of the earth shall be blessed."

GENESIS 12:1-3 NASB

All the ends of the earth will remember and turn to the Lord, and all the families of the nations will worship before You. For the kingdom is the Lord's, and He rules over the nations.

PSALM 22:27,28 NASB

After these things I looked, and behold, a great multitude which no one could count, from every nation and all tribes and peoples and tongues, standing before the throne and before the Lamb, clothed in white robes, and palm branches were in their hands.

REVELATION 7:9 NASB

PROMISES

They will be my people, and I will be their God. And I will give them one heart and mind to worship me forever, for their own good and for the good of all their descendants. And I will make an everlasting covenant with them, promising not to stop doing good for them.

JEREMIAH 32:38-40 NLT

Behold, children are a gift of the Lord, the fruit of the womb is a reward.

PSALM 127:3 NASB

Like a warrior's fistful of arrows are the children of a vigorous youth. Oh, how blessed are you parents, with your quivers full of children!

PSALM 127:4,5 THE MESSAGE

Children's children are a crown to the aged, and parents are the pride of their children.

PROVERBS 17:6 NIV

The father of godly children has cause for joy.
What a pleasure it is to have wise children.

PROVERBS 23:24 NLT

Correct your son, and he will give you rest;
Yes, he will give delight to your soul.

PROVERBS 29:17 NKJV

EXAMPLE

*God chose Abraham to be His covenant partner
because He trusted Abraham to discipline his children and teach them to do right. Abraham gave the
Lord godly offspring through which He could then
bless all the nations of the earth:*

For I know him, that he will command his
children and his household after him, and they
shall keep the way of the Lord, to do justice
and judgment; that the Lord may bring upon
Abraham that which he hath spoken of him.

GENESIS 18:19 KJV

———◇◇◇———

Q: LORD, HOW SHOULD
I PRAY FOR MY CHILDREN?
PLEASE TEACH ME!

———◇◇◇———

A: "This is what I want you to do: Ask the
Father for whatever is in keeping with the
things I've revealed to you. Ask in my name,
according to my will, and he'll most certainly
give it to you."   JOHN 16:23,24 THE MESSAGE

Rise during the night and cry out. Pour out
your hearts like water to the Lord. Lift up your
hands to him in prayer. Plead for your children.

LAMENTATIONS 2:19 NLT

INSTRUCTIONS

Keep on asking, and you will be given what
you ask for. Keep on looking, and you will find.
Keep on knocking, and the door will be
opened. For everyone who asks, receives.
Everyone who seeks, finds. And the door is

opened to everyone who knocks. You parents
— if your children ask for a loaf of bread, do
you give them a stone instead? Or if they ask
for a fish, do you give them a snake? Of course
not! If you sinful people know how to give
good gifts to your children, how much more
will your heavenly Father give good gifts to
those who ask him.

MATTHEW 7:7-11 NLT

I am the vine, and you are the branches. If you
stay joined to me, and I stay joined to you,
then you will produce lots of fruit. But you
cannot do anything without me. Stay joined to
me and let my teachings become part of you.
Then you can pray for whatever you want, and
your prayer will be answered.

JOHN 15:5,7 CEV

God is strong, and he wants you strong. So
take everything the Master has set out for you,
well-made weapons of the best materials. And
put them to use so you will be able to stand up
to everything the Devil throws your way. This
is no afternoon athletic contest that we'll walk
away from and forget about in a couple of
hours. This is for keeps, a life-or-death fight to
the finish against the Devil and all his angels.

Be prepared. You're up against far more than
you can handle on your own. Take all the help
you can get, every weapon God has issued, so
that when it's all over but the shouting you'll
still be on your feet.... God's Word is an *indis-
pensable* weapon. In the same way, prayer is
essential in this ongoing warfare. Pray hard and
long.
                         EPHESIANS 6:10-18 THE MESSAGE

Never give up praying. And when you pray,
keep alert and be thankful.
                              COLOSSIANS 4:2 CEV

Always pray by the power of the Spirit.

                                   EPHESIANS 6:18 CEV

The Holy Spirit helps us in our distress. For
we don't even know what we should pray for,
nor how we should pray. But the Holy Spirit
prays for us with groanings that cannot be
expressed in words. And the Father who knows
all hearts knows what the Spirit is saying, for
the Spirit pleads for us believers in harmony
with God's own will.
                               ROMANS 8:26,27 NLT

I will pray with the spirit, and I will also pray
with the understanding.

                             1 CORINTHIANS 14:15 NKJV

PROMISES

Then said the Lord to me...I am alert and active, watching over My word to perform it.

JEREMIAH 1:12 AMP

This is the confidence which we have before Him, that, if we ask anything according to His will, He hears us. And if we know that He hears us in whatever we ask, we know that we have the requests which we have asked from Him.

1 JOHN 5:14,15 NASB

And Jesus replying said to them, Have faith in God (constantly). Truly, I tell you, whoever says to this mountain, Be lifted up and thrown into the sea! and does not doubt at all in his heart, but believes that what he says will take place, it will be done for him. For this reason I am telling you, whatever you ask for in prayer, believe — trust and be confident — that it is granted to you, and you will [get it].

MARK 11:22-24 AMP

Let us then fearlessly and confidently and boldly draw near to the throne of grace...that we may receive mercy...and find grace to help

in good time for every need — appropriate
help and well-timed help, coming just when
we need it.

HEBREWS 4:16 AMP

The earnest (heartfelt, continued) prayer of a
righteous man makes tremendous power available — dynamic in its working.

JAMES 5:16 AMP

With God's power working in us, God can do
much, much more than anything we can ask or
imagine.

EPHESIANS 3:20 NCV

TO PRAY FOR YOUR CHILD

I pray that Christ will live in your hearts by
faith and that your life will be strong in love
and be built on love. And I pray that you...will
have the power to understand the greatness of
Christ's love — how wide and how long and
how high and how deep that love is. Christ's
love is greater than anyone can ever know, but
I pray that you will be able to know that love.
Then you can be filled with the fullness of
God.

EPHESIANS 3:17-19 NCV

We ask God to give you a complete under-standing of what he wants to do in your lives, and we ask him to make you wise with spiritual wisdom. Then the way you live will always honor and please the Lord, and you will continually do good, kind things for others...We also pray that you will be strengthened with his glorious power so that you will have all the patience and endurance you need. May you be filled with joy, always thanking the Father.

COLOSSIANS 1:9-12 NLT

Father...keep them safe from the evil one.

JOHN 17:15 CEV

EXAMPLES

Hannah, Samuel's mother, poured her heart out to God, asking Him for a child. After her prayer was answered, she dedicated her son to the Lord:

"For this boy I prayed, and the Lord has given me my petition which I asked of Him. So I have also dedicated him to the Lord; as long as he lives he is dedicated to the Lord."

1 SAMUEL 1:27,28 NASB

Q: HOW CAN I BE MORE LOVING TO MY FAMILY?

A: Watch what God does, and then you do it, like children who learn proper behavior from their parents. Mostly what God does is love you. Keep company with him and learn a life of love. Observe how Christ loved us. His love was not cautious but extravagant. He didn't love in order to get something from us but to give everything of himself to us. Love like that.

EPHESIANS 5:1,2 THE MESSAGE

You must quit being angry, hateful, and evil. You must no longer say insulting or cruel things about others. And stop lying to each other. You have given up your old way of life with its habits. Each of you is now a new person. You are becoming more and more like your Creator.... So be gentle, kind, humble, meek, and patient. Put up with each other, and forgive anyone who does you wrong, just as

Christ has forgiven you.

COLOSSIANS 3:8-10,12,13 CEV

Above all things have fervent love for one another, for "love will cover a multitude of sins."

1 PETER 4:8 NKJV

All who proclaim that Jesus is the Son of God have God living in them, and they live in God.... As we live in God, our love grows more perfect. We love each other as a result of his loving us first.

1 JOHN 4:15,17,19 NLT

Give as freely as you have received!

MATTHEW 10:8 NLT

Love endures long and is patient and kind; love never is envious nor boils over with jealousy; is not boastful or vainglorious, does not display itself haughtily. It is not conceited — arrogant and inflated with pride; it is not rude (unmannerly), and does not act unbecomingly. Love [God's love in us] does not insist on its own rights or its own way, for it is not self-seeking; it is not touchy or fretful or resentful; it takes no account of the evil done to it — pays no attention to a suffered wrong. It does not rejoice at injustice and unrighteousness, but rejoices when right and truth prevail. Love bears up under anything and everything that comes, is ever ready to believe the best of every person, its hopes are fadeless under all circumstances and it endures everything [without weakening]. Love never fails — never fades out or becomes obsolete or comes to an end.

1 CORINTHIANS 13:4-8 AMP

PROMISES

When the Holy Spirit controls our lives, he will produce this kind of fruit in us: love, joy, peace, patience, kindness, goodness, faithfulness, gentleness, and self-control.

GALATIANS 5:22,23 NLT

God has poured out his love into our hearts by the Holy Spirit, whom he has given us.

ROMANS 5:5 NIV

God is not unjust; he will not forget your work and the love you have shown him as you have helped his people and continue to help them.

HEBREWS 6:10 NIV

PRAYER

May the Lord make your love increase and overflow for each other and for everyone else, just as ours does for you.

1 THESSALONIANS 3:12 NIV

I pray that the Lord will guide you to be as loving as God and as patient as Christ.

2 THESSALONIANS 3:5 CEV

We pray that our Lord Jesus Christ and God our Father will encourage you and help you always to do and say the right thing.

2 THESSALONIANS 2:16,17 CEV

May your roots go down deep into the soil of God's marvelous love. And may you have the power to understand...how wide, how long, how high, and how deep his love really is. May you experience the love of Christ, though it is so great you will never fully understand it. Then you will be filled with the fullness of life and power that comes from God.

EPHESIANS 3:17-19 NLT

We also pray that you will be strengthened

with his glorious power so that you will have all the patience and endurance you need.

COLOSSIANS 1:11 NLT

I pray that your love for each other will overflow more and more, and that you will keep on growing in your knowledge and understanding. For I want you to understand what really matters, so that you may live pure and blameless lives until Christ returns. May you always be filled with the fruit of your salvation — those good things that are produced in your life by Jesus Christ.

PHILIPPIANS 1:9-11 NLT

EXAMPLE

God gave us the ultimate example of love:

This is how God showed his love for us: God sent his only Son into the world so we might live through him.... If God loved us like this, we certainly ought to love each other.

1 JOHN 4:9,11 THE MESSAGE

If we love each other, God lives in us, and his love has been brought to full expression through us.

1 JOHN 4:12 NLT

Q: LORD, SO MANY
DECISIONS FACE ME DAILY —
WHERE CAN A MOTHER TURN FOR
DIRECTION AND GUIDANCE?

A: If you need wisdom — if you want to
know what God wants you to do — ask him,
and he will gladly tell you.

JAMES 1:5 NLT

INSTRUCTIONS

Call to me and I will answer you and tell you
great and unsearchable things you do not
know.

JEREMIAH 33:3 NIV

My child, listen to me and treasure my
instructions. Tune your ears to wisdom, and
concentrate on understanding.... Search for
them as you would for lost money or hidden
treasure. Then you will understand what it
means to fear the Lord, and you will gain
knowledge of God.

PROVERBS 2:1,2,4,5 NLT

Trust God from the bottom of your heart.
Don't try to figure out everything on your own.
Listen for God's voice in everything you do,
everywhere you go. He's the one who will keep
you on track. Don't assume that you know it
all. Run to God!

PROVERBS 3:5-7 THE MESSAGE

All Scripture is inspired by God and is useful
to teach us what is true and to make us realize
what is wrong in our lives. It straightens us out
and teaches us to do what is right. It is God's
way of preparing us in every way, fully
equipped for every good thing God wants us to
do.

2 TIMOTHY 3:16,17 NLT

PROMISES

He will feed His flock like a shepherd; He
will gather the lambs with His arm, and carry
them in His bosom, and gently lead those who
are with young.

ISAIAH 40:11 NKJV

I will instruct you and teach you in the way
you should go; I will counsel you and watch
over you.

PSALM 32:8 NIV

Your word is a lamp to my feet and a light to my path.

PSALM 119:105 NKJV

The statutes of the Lord are trustworthy, making wise the simple. The precepts of the Lord are right, giving joy to the heart. The commands of the Lord are radiant, giving light to the eyes. By them is your servant warned; in keeping them there is great reward.

PSALM 19:7,8,11 NIV

PRAYERS

Send forth your light and your truth, let them guide me.

PSALM 43:3 NIV

Show me the path where I should walk, O Lord; point out the right road for me to follow. Lead me by your truth and teach me, for you are the God who saves me. All day long I put my hope in you.

PSALM 25:4,5 NLT

Teach me to do your will, for you are my God. May your gracious Spirit lead me forward on a firm footing.

PSALM 143:10 NLT

"Give me an understanding mind so that I can govern your people well and know the difference between what is right and what is wrong. For who by himself is able to carry such a heavy responsibility?"

1 KINGS 3:9 TLB

I will bless the Lord who guides me; even at night my heart instructs me.

PSALM 16:7 NLT

Your statutes are my delight; they are my counselors.

PSALM 119:24 NIV

EXAMPLE

When an enemy army came against Jehoshaphat, he sought the Lord for wisdom and guidance:

"We have no power to face this vast army that is attacking us. We do not know what to do, but our eyes are upon you." Then the Spirit of the Lord came upon Jahaziel.... He said..."This is what the Lord says to you: 'Do not be afraid or discouraged because of this vast army. For the battle is not yours, but God's. Go out to face them tomorrow, and the Lord will be with you.'"

2 CHRONICLES 20:12,14,15,17 NIV

Q: SOMETIMES THE KIDS ARE
JUST TOO MUCH FOR ME!
IS THERE A WAY TO KEEP MY JOY,
NO MATTER WHAT HAPPENS?

A: You are my hiding place! You protect me from trouble, and you put songs in my heart.

PSALM 32:7 CEV

I was pushed back and about to fall, but the Lord helped me. The Lord is my strength and my song; he has become my salvation.

PSALM 118:13,14 NIV

INSTRUCTIONS

Let all who take refuge in you be glad; let them ever sing for joy. Spread your protection over them, that those who love your name may rejoice in you. For surely, O Lord, you bless the righteous; you surround them with your favor as with a shield.

PSALM 5:11,12 NIV

Let the godly rejoice. Let them be glad in God's presence. Let them be filled with joy.

Sing praises to God and to his name! Sing loud praises to him who rides the clouds. His name is the Lord — rejoice in his presence!

PSALM 68:3,4 NLT

Let the heavens rejoice, and let the earth be glad; and let them say among the nations, "The Lord reigns." Oh, give thanks to the Lord, for He is good! For His mercy endures forever.

1 CHRONICLES 16:31,34 NKJV

Celebrate God all day, every day. I mean, revel in him!

PHILIPPIANS 4:4 THE MESSAGE

Speak to each other with psalms, hymns, and spiritual songs, singing and making music in your hearts to the Lord. Always give thanks to God the Father for everything, in the name of our Lord Jesus Christ.

EPHESIANS 5:19,20 NCV

And you shall rejoice before the Lord your God in all that you undertake.

DEUTERONOMY 12:18 AMP

Do everything without complaining.

PHILIPPIANS 2:14 NCV

Dear brothers and sisters, whenever trouble comes your way, let it be an opportunity for joy. For when your faith is tested, your endurance has a chance to grow. So let it grow, for when your endurance is fully developed, you will be strong in character and ready for anything.

JAMES 1:2-4 NLT

Though you have not seen him, you love him; and even though you do not see him now, you believe in him and are filled with an inexpressible and glorious joy.

1 PETER 1:8 NIV

PRAYERS

I will sing to the Lord as long as I live; I will sing praise to my God while I have my being. May my meditation be sweet to Him; I will be glad in the Lord.

PSALM 104:33,34 NKJV

I will greatly rejoice in the Lord, my soul shall be joyful in my God; for He has clothed me with the garments of salvation, He has covered me with the robe of righteousness, as...a bride adorns herself with her jewels.

Isaiah 61:10 NKJV

It is good to say, "thank you" to the Lord, to sing praises to the God who is above all gods. Every morning tell him, "Thank you for your kindness," and every evening rejoice in all his faithfulness. You have done so much for me, O Lord. No wonder I am glad! I sing for joy.

Psalm 92:1,2,4 TLB

Why are you cast down, O my inner self? And why should you moan over me and be disquieted within me? Hope in God and wait expectantly for Him; for I shall yet praise Him, Who is the help of my [sad] countenance, and my God.

Psalm 43:5 AMP

PROMISES

Though a righteous man falls seven times, he rises again.

Proverbs 24:16 NIV

Blessed, happy, to be envied is the man who is patient under trial and stands up under temptation, for when he has stood the test and been approved he will receive [the victor's] crown of life which God has promised to those who love Him.

JAMES 1:12 AMP

We also have joy with our troubles, because we know that these troubles produce patience. And patience produces character, and character produces hope. And this hope will never disappoint us, because God has poured out his love to fill our hearts.

ROMANS 5:3-5 NCV

EXAMPLE

Just after God warns him of an impending invasion, Habakkuk declares that his joy is not based on his circumstances but in his God:

Fig trees may not grow figs. There may be no grapes on the vines. There may be no olives growing on the trees. There may be no food growing in the fields. There may be no sheep in the pens. There may be no cattle in the barns. But I will still be glad in the Lord. I will rejoice in God my Savior. The Lord God gives me my strength.

HABAKKUK 3:17-19 ICB

Q: LORD, I'VE PRAYED FOR MY CHILD BUT I DON'T SEE ANY CHANGES. WHAT SHOULD I DO?

A: Trust in the Lord, and do good; dwell in the land, and feed on His faithfulness. Delight yourself also in the Lord, and He shall give you the desires of your heart. Commit your way to the Lord, trust also in Him, and He shall bring it to pass. Rest in the Lord, and wait patiently for Him.

PSALM 37:3-5,7 NKJV

INSTRUCTIONS

You need to persevere so that when you have done the will of God, you will receive what he has promised.

HEBREWS 10:36 NIV

Therefore, take up the full armor of God, so that you may be able to resist in the evil day, and having done everything, to stand firm.

EPHESIANS 6:13 NASB

Stand firm. Let nothing move you. Always give yourselves fully to the work of the Lord, because you know that your labor in the Lord is not in vain.

1 CORINTHIANS 15:58 NIV

Wait...for God. Wait with hope. Hope now; hope always!

PSALM 131:3 THE MESSAGE

"Have faith in God," Jesus answered. "I tell you the truth, if anyone says to this mountain, 'Go, throw yourself into the sea,' and does not doubt in his heart but believes that what he says will happen, it will be done for him. Therefore I tell you, whatever you ask for in prayer, believe that you have received it, and it will be yours."

MARK 11:22-24 NIV

We're not giving up. How could we! Even though on the outside it often looks like things are falling apart on us, on the inside, where God is making new life, not a day goes by without his unfolding grace.... There's far more here than meets the eye. The things we see now are here today, gone tomorrow. But the things we can't see now will last forever.

2 CORINTHIANS 4:16,18 THE MESSAGE

Be like those who through faith and patience will receive what God has promised.

HEBREWS 6:12 NCV

Stay with God! Take heart. Don't quit. I'll say it again: Stay with God.

PSALM 27:14 THE MESSAGE

PRAYERS

May the God of hope fill you with all joy and peace as you trust in him, so that you may overflow with hope by the power of the Holy Spirit.

ROMANS 15:13 NIV

We pray that you'll have the strength to stick it out over the long haul — not the grim strength of gritting your teeth but the glory-strength God gives. It is strength that endures the unendurable and spills over into joy.

COLOSSIANS 1:11 THE MESSAGE

PROMISES

Everything that was written in the past was written to teach us. The Scriptures give us patience and encouragement so that we can have hope. Patience and encouragement come from God.

ROMANS 15:4,5 NCV

He gives power to the faint and weary, and to him who has no might He increases strength — causing it to multiply and making it abound...Those who wait for the Lord — who expect, look for and hope in Him — shall change and renew their strength and power; they shall lift their wings and mount up [close to God] as eagles [mount up to the sun]; they shall run and not be weary; they shall walk and not faint or become tired.

ISAIAH 40:29,31 AMP

Don't worry about anything; instead, pray about everything. Tell God what you need, and thank him for all he has done. If you do this, you will experience God's peace, which is far more wonderful than the human mind can understand. His peace will guard your hearts and minds as you live in Christ Jesus.

PHILIPPIANS 4:6,7 NLT

The earnest (heartfelt, continued) prayer of a righteous man makes tremendous power available — dynamic in its working.

JAMES 5:16 AMP

When God made his promise to Abraham, he backed it to the hilt, putting his own reputation on the line. He said, "I promise that I'll bless you with everything I have — bless and bless and bless!" Abraham stuck it out and got everything that had been promised to him. When God wanted to guarantee his promises, he gave his word, a rock-solid guarantee — God can't break his word. And because his word cannot change, the promise is likewise unchangeable. We who have run for our very lives to God have every reason to grab the promised hope with both hands and never let go. It's an unbreakable spiritual lifeline, reaching past all appearances right to the very presence of God.

HEBREWS 6:13,14,17-19 THE MESSAGE

We continue to shout our praise even when we're hemmed in with troubles, because we know how troubles can develop passionate patience in us, and how that patience in turn forges the tempered steel of virtue, keeping us alert for whatever God will do next.

ROMANS 5:3,4 THE MESSAGE

EXAMPLE

Abraham kept believing God's promise to him, no matter what he saw or felt:

There was no hope that Abraham would have children. But Abraham believed God and continued hoping, and so he became the father of many nations. As God told him, "Your descendants also will be too many to count." Abraham was almost a hundred years old, much past the age for having children, and Sarah could not have children. Abraham thought about all this, but his faith in God did not become weak. He never doubted that God would keep his promise, and he never stopped believing. He grew stronger in his faith and gave praise to God. Abraham felt sure that God was able to do what he had promised.

ROMANS 4:18-21 NCV

And so after waiting patiently, Abraham received what was promised. HEBREWS 6:15 NIV

—∞—

Q: Good parents give consistent discipline. How can I get better at this?

—∞—

A: Discipline your children; you'll be glad you did — they'll turn out delightful to live with.

PROVERBS 29:17 THE MESSAGE

A refusal to correct is a refusal to love; love your children by disciplining them.

PROVERBS 13:24 THE MESSAGE

INSTRUCTIONS

Teach a child to choose the right path, and when he is older he will remain upon it.

PROVERBS 22:6 TLB

Do not provoke your children to anger, but bring them up in the discipline and instruction of the Lord.

EPHESIANS 6:4 NASB

All Scripture is given by God and is useful for

teaching, for showing people what is wrong in their lives, for correcting faults, and for teaching how to live right. Using the Scriptures, the person who serves God will be capable, having all that is needed to do every good work.

2 TIMOTHY 3:16,17 NCV

Don't exasperate your children by coming down hard on them. Take them by the hand and lead them in the way of the Master.

EPHESIANS 6:4 THE MESSAGE

Don't fail to correct your children. They won't die if you spank them. Physical discipline may well save them from death.

PROVERBS 23:13,14 NLT

Foolishness is bound up in the heart of a child; the rod of correction will drive it far from him.

PROVERBS 22:15 NKJV

The rod of correction imparts wisdom, but a child left to himself disgraces his mother.

PROVERBS 29:15 NIV

INSTRUCTIONS FOR YOUR CHILD

You are living a brand new kind of life that is continually learning more and more of what is right, and trying constantly to be more and more like Christ who created this new life within you. Remember what Christ taught and let his words enrich your lives and make you wise.

COLOSSIANS 3:10,16 TLB

Since you were a child you have known the Holy Scriptures which are able to make you wise. And that wisdom leads to salvation through faith in Christ Jesus.

2 TIMOTHY 3:15 NCV

My children, listen to your father's teaching. Pay attention so you will understand.... Do not forget what I teach you. I was once a young boy in my father's house. I was like an only child to my mother. And my father taught me and said, "Hold on to my words with all your heart. Keep my commands and you will live. Get wisdom and understanding. Don't forget or ignore my words. Use wisdom, and it will take care of you. Love wisdom, and it will keep

you safe. Wisdom is the most important thing.
So get wisdom. If it costs everything you have,
get understanding.

PROVERBS 4:1-7 ICB

It is never fun to be corrected. In fact, at the
time it is always painful. But if we learn to
obey by being corrected, we will do right and
live at peace.

HEBREWS 12:11 CEV

A person who refuses correction will end up
poor and disgraced. But a person who accepts
correction will be honored.

PROVERBS 13:18 ICB

Only a fool despises a parent's discipline;
whoever learns from correction is wise.

PROVERBS 15:5 NLT

Children, obey your parents; this is the right
thing to do because God has placed them in
authority over you. Honor your father and
mother. This is the first of God's Ten
Commandments that ends with a promise.
And this is the promise: that if you honor your
father and mother, yours will be a long life, full
of blessing.

EPHESIANS 6:1-3 TLB

EXAMPLE

God, the ultimate Father, disciplines His children with love, patience, and consistency:

"My child, don't think the Lord's discipline is worth nothing, and don't stop trying when he corrects you. The Lord disciplines those he loves, and he punishes everyone he accepts as his child."
So hold on through your sufferings, because they are like a father's discipline. God is treating you as children. All children are disciplined by their fathers. If you are never disciplined (and every child must be disciplined), you are not true children.
Our fathers on earth disciplined us for a short time in the way they thought was best. But God disciplines us to help us, so we can become holy as he is. We do not enjoy being disciplined. It is painful, but later, after we have learned from it, we have peace, because we start living in the right way.

HEBREWS 12:5-8,10,11 NCV

—∞◇∞—

Q: HOW CAN I CONTROL
MY TEMPER AND BE MORE
PATIENT WITH MY CHILD?

—∞◇∞—

A: Those who control their anger have great understanding; those with a hasty temper will make mistakes.

PROVERBS 14:29 NLT

Slowness to anger makes for deep understanding; a quick-tempered person stockpiles stupidity.

PROVERBS 14:29 THE MESSAGE

INSTRUCTIONS

Put these things out of your life: anger, bad temper, doing or saying things to hurt others, and using evil words when you talk.

COLOSSIANS 3:8 NCV

I promise you that on the day of judgment, everyone will have to account for every careless word they have spoken.

MATTHEW 12:36 CEV

"You're familiar with the command to the ancients, 'Do not murder.' I'm telling you that anyone who is so much as angry with a brother or sister is guilty of murder.... The simple moral fact is that words kill."

MATTHEW 5:21,22 THE MESSAGE

"Don't sin by letting anger gain control over you." Don't let the sun go down while you are still angry, for anger gives a mighty foothold to the Devil.

EPHESIANS 4:26,27 NLT

When you talk, do not say harmful things, but say what people need — words that will help others become stronger. Then what you say will do good to those who listen to you.

EPHESIANS 4:29 NCV

Let every man be quick to hear, (a ready listener,) slow to speak, slow to take offense and to get angry.

JAMES 1:19 AMP

God's righteousness doesn't grow from human anger.

JAMES 1:20 THE MESSAGE

Do not be overcome by evil, but overcome evil with good.

ROMANS 12:21 NASB

Since God chose you to be the holy people whom he loves, you must clothe yourselves with tenderhearted mercy, kindness, humility, gentleness, and patience. You must make allowance for each other's faults and forgive the person who offends you. Remember, the Lord forgave you, so you must forgive others.

COLOSSIANS 3:12,13 NLT

PROMISES

We have everything we need to live a life that pleases God. It was all given to us by God's own power, when we learned that he had invited us to share in his wonderful goodness. God made great and marvelous promises, so that his nature would become part of us.

2 PETER 1:3,4 CEV

So make every effort to apply the benefits of these promises to your life.... Knowing God leads to self-control. Self-control leads to patient endurance, and patient endurance leads to godliness.

2 PETER 1:5,6 NLT

"Blessed are the merciful, for they shall receive mercy.... Blessed are the peacemakers, for they shall be called sons of God."

MATTHEW 5:7,9 NASB

Delight yourself also in the Lord, and He will give you the desires and secret petitions of your heart. Commit your way to the Lord — roll and repose [each care of] your load on Him; trust (lean on, rely on and be confident) also in Him, and He will bring it to pass. Be still and rest in the Lord; wait for Him, and patiently stay yourself upon Him.... Cease from anger and forsake wrath; fret not yourself; it tends only to evil-doing.... But the meek [in the end] shall inherit the earth, and shall delight themselves in the abundance of peace.

PSALM 37:4,5,7,8,11 AMP

PRAYER

Who can understand his errors? Cleanse me from secret faults. Keep back Your servant also from presumptuous sins; let them not have dominion over me. Then I shall be blameless, and I shall be innocent of great transgression. Let the words of my mouth and the meditation of my heart be acceptable in Your sight, O

Lord, my strength and my Redeemer.

PSALM 19:12-14 NKJV

We always pray that God will show you everything he wants you to do and that you may have all the wisdom and understanding that his Spirit gives. Then you will live a life that honors the Lord.

COLOSSIANS 1:9,10 CEV

EXAMPLE

Our Heavenly Father sees our failures and weakness yet responds with mercy and not anger.

The Lord is merciful and gracious, slow to anger, and plenteous in mercy and loving-kindness. He will not always chide or be contending, neither will He keep His anger for ever or hold a grudge. He has not dealt with us after our sins, nor rewarded us according to our iniquities.... As a father loves and pities his children, so the Lord loves and pities those who fear Him — with reverence, worship and awe. For He knows our frame; He [earnestly] remembers and imprints [on His heart] that we are dust.

PSALM 103:8-10,13,14 AMP

◇◇◇

Q: LORD, HOW CAN I STOP WORRYING ABOUT MY CHILDREN'S SAFETY? WILL YOU PROTECT THEM WHEN I'M NOT THERE?

◇◇◇

A: If you respect the Lord, you and your children have a strong fortress and a life-giving fountain that keeps you safe from deadly traps.

PROVERBS 14:26,27 CEV

Those who know Your name will put their trust in You; for You, Lord, have not forsaken those who seek You.

PSALM 9:10 NKJV

INSTRUCTIONS

Don't fret or worry. Instead of worrying, pray. Let petitions and praises shape your worries into prayers, letting God know your concerns. Before you know it, a sense of God's whole-ness, everything coming together for good, will come and settle you down. It's wonderful what happens when Christ displaces worry at the center of your life.

PHILIPPIANS 4:6-8 THE MESSAGE

Cast your burden on the Lord, and He shall sustain you; He will never permit the righteous to be moved.

PSALM 55:22 NKJV

Casting the whole of your care — all your anxieties, all your worries, all your concerns, once and for all — on Him; for He cares for you affectionately, and cares about you watchfully.

1 PETER 5:7 AMP

PROMISES

I am leaving you with a gift — peace of mind and heart. And the peace I give isn't like the peace the world gives. So don't be troubled or afraid.

JOHN 14:27 NLT

The Lord is my light and my salvation; whom shall I fear or dread? The Lord is the refuge and stronghold of my life; of whom shall I be afraid?

PSALM 27:1 AMP

In righteousness you shall be established; you

shall be far from oppression, for you shall not
fear; and from terror, for it shall not come near
you.

ISAIAH 54:14 NKJV

Those who live in the shelter of the Most
High will find rest in the shadow of the
Almighty. This I declare of the Lord; He alone
is my refuge, my place of safety; he is my God,
and I am trusting him.

PSALM 91:1,2 NLT

You are my hiding place; you will protect me
from trouble and surround me with songs of
deliverance. Selah.

PSALM 32:7 NIV

PROMISES FOR YOUR CHILD

For he will rescue you from every trap and protect you from the fatal plague. He will shield
you with his wings.... His faithful promises are
your armor and protection.

Do not be afraid of the terrors of the night,
nor fear the dangers of the day.... Though a
thousand fall at your side, though ten thousand
are dying around you, these evils will not touch
you. For he orders his angels to protect you
wherever you go.

PSALM 91:3-5,7,11 NLT

The Lord says, "I will rescue those who love me. I will protect those who trust in my name. When they call on me, I will answer; I will be with them in trouble. I will rescue them and honor them. I will satisfy them with a long life and give them my salvation."

PSALM 91:14-16 NLT

But the Lord is faithful, and he will strengthen and protect you from the evil one.

2 THESSALONIANS 3:3 NIV

The angel of the Lord encamps around those who fear Him, and rescues them.

PSALM 34:7 NASB

PRAYERS

May the God of hope fill you with all joy and peace as you trust in him, so that you may overflow with hope by the power of the Holy Spirit.

ROMANS 15:13 NIV

In the multitude of my (anxious) thoughts
within me, Your comforts cheer and delight my
soul!

PSALM 94:19 AMP

EXAMPLE

*Pharaoh hardened his heart and refused to let the
children of Israel go free. Moses warned him: "Every
firstborn son in Egypt will die" (Exodus 11:5 NIV).
But Pharaoh did not heed the warning.*

Then Moses summoned all the elders of Israel
and said to them, "Go at once and...slaughter
the Passover lamb. Take a bunch of hyssop, dip
it into the blood in the basin and put some of
the blood on the top and on both sides of the
doorframe. Not one of you shall go out the door
of his house until morning. When the Lord goes
through the land...he will see the blood...and
will pass over that doorway, and he will not
permit the destroyer to enter your houses and
strike you down."

EXODUS 12:21-23 NIV

*There was a death in every Egyptian house. But
among God's people, every child was protected
because of the faith and obedience of their parents.*

Q: HOW CAN I COMMUNICATE
— HEART TO HEART —
WITH MY CHILD?

A: My dear brothers and sisters, always be
willing to listen and slow to speak.

JAMES 1:19 NCV

INSTRUCTIONS

Listen carefully to what you hear! The way
you treat others will be the way you will be
treated.

MARK 4:24 CEV

When others are happy, be happy with them.
If they are sad, share their sorrow.

ROMANS 12:15 NLT

The purposes of a man's heart are deep waters,
but a man of understanding draws them out.

PROVERBS 20:5 NIV

The heart of the discerning acquires knowledge; the ears of the wise seek it out.

PROVERBS 18:15 NIV

Let the wise listen and add to their learning.

PROVERBS 1:5 NIV

PROMISES

Through skillful and godly Wisdom is a house [a life, a home, a family] built, and by understanding it is established [on a sound and good foundation]. And by knowledge shall the chambers [of its every area] be filled with all precious and pleasant riches.

PROVERBS 24:3,4 AMP

EXAMPLE

Time spent with children is never wasted:

Jesus called a little child to him...Then he said..."The greatest person in the kingdom of heaven is the one who makes himself humble like this child. Whoever accepts a child in my name accepts me."

MATTHEW 18:2-5 NCV

Q: MY PARENTS WERE CRITICAL
OF ME — AND I FIND MYSELF
BEING CRITICAL OF MY CHILD.
HOW CAN I BREAK THIS CYCLE?

INSTRUCTIONS

Let everything you say be good and helpful, so that your words will be an encouragement to those who hear them.

EPHESIANS 4:29 NLT

Say only what helps, each word a gift.

EPHESIANS 4:29 THE MESSAGE

When you talk, do not say harmful things, but say what people need — words that will help others become stronger.

EPHESIANS 4:29 NCV

"Be easy on people; you'll find life a lot easier."

LUKE 6:37 THE MESSAGE

Be quick to listen, slow to speak, and slow to

get angry. Your anger can never make things right in God's sight.

JAMES 1:19,20 NLT

There is one who speaks rashly like the thrusts of a sword, but the tongue of the wise brings healing.

PROVERBS 12:18 NASB

"Don't pick on people, jump on their failures, criticize their faults — unless, of course, you want the same treatment. That critical spirit has a way of boomeranging."

MATTHEW 7:1 THE MESSAGE

If you think you can judge others, you are wrong. When you judge them, you are really judging yourself guilty, because you do the same things they do.

ROMANS 2:1 NCV

PROMISES

You shall call, and the Lord will answer; you shall cry, and He will say, Here I am. If you take away from your midst yokes of oppression [wherever you find them], the finger pointed in scorn...and every form of false, harsh, unjust and wicked speaking; and if you pour out that with which you sustain your own life for the hungry, and satisfy the need of the afflicted, then shall your light rise in darkness and your obscurity and gloom be as the noonday.

And the Lord shall guide you continually, and satisfy you in drought and in dry places, and make strong your bones. And you shall be like a watered garden and like a spring of water, whose waters fail not. And your ancient ruins shall be rebuilt; you shall raise up the foundations of...many generations; and you shall be called the repairer of the breach, the restorer of streets to dwell in.

ISAIAH 58:9-12 AMP

The Lord God hath given me the tongue of the learned, that I should know how to speak a word in season to him that is weary: he wakeneth morning by morning, he wakeneth mine ear to hear as the learned.

ISAIAH 50:4 KJV

PRAYERS

"Teach me, and I will hold my tongue; cause me to understand wherein I have erred."

JOB 6:24 NKJV

"I will guard my ways, lest I sin with my tongue; I will restrain my mouth with a muzzle."

PSALM 39:1 NKJV

Who can understand his errors? Cleanse me from secret faults.

PSALM 19:12 NKJV

Now may the God of peace...Strengthen (complete, perfect) and make you what you ought to be, and equip you with everything good that you may carry out His will; [while He Himself] works in you and accomplishes that which is pleasing in His sight, through Jesus Christ.

HEBREWS 13:20,21 AMP

EXAMPLE

Proverbs 31 gives us a profile of a virtuous woman, wife, and mother. When she speaks, her words build up and encourage her family:

She opens her mouth with wisdom, and on her tongue is the law of kindness. Her children rise up and call her blessed; her husband also, and he praises her: "Many daughters have done well, but you excel them all."

PROVERBS 31:26,28,29 NKJV

Q: MY CHILD IS WITHDRAWING
FROM ME. HOW CAN I
RESTORE CLOSENESS IN
OUR RELATIONSHIP?

A: "In repentance and rest is your salvation,
in quietness and trust is your strength."

ISAIAH 30:15 NIV

A kind answer soothes angry feelings, but
harsh words stir them up.

PROVERBS 15:1 CEV

INSTRUCTIONS

It is harder to win back the friendship of an
offended brother than to capture a fortified
city. His anger shuts you out like iron bars.

PROVERBS 18:19 TLB

Stay away from foolish and stupid arguments,
because you know they grow into quarrels. And
a servant of the Lord must not quarrel but

must be kind to everyone, a good teacher, and patient. The Lord's servant must gently teach those who disagree.

2 TIMOTHY 2:23-25 NCV

All of you should be of one mind, full of sympathy toward each other, loving one another with tender hearts and humble minds. Don't repay evil for evil. Don't retaliate when people say unkind things about you. Instead, pay them back with a blessing. That's what God wants you to do, and he will bless you for it.

1 PETER 3:8,9 NLT

Be quick to listen and slow to speak or to get angry.

JAMES 1:19 CEV

Let's agree to use all our energy in getting along with each other. Help others with encouraging words; don't drag them down by finding fault.

ROMANS 14:19 THE MESSAGE

Rejoice with those who rejoice; mourn with those who mourn. Live in harmony with one another.

ROMANS 12:15,16 NIV

Confess your sins to each other and pray for each other so that you can live together whole and healed. The prayer of a person living right with God is something powerful to be reckoned with.

JAMES 5:16 THE MESSAGE

He who covers his transgressions will not prosper, but whoever confesses and forsakes his sins shall obtain mercy.

PROVERBS 28:13 AMP

PROMISES

"For I am the Lord your God, who upholds your right hand, Who says to you, 'Do not fear, I will help you.'"

ISAIAH 41:13 NASB

He will turn the hearts of the fathers to their children, and the hearts of the children to their fathers.

MALACHI 4:6 NIV

I will instruct you and teach you in the way you should go; I will counsel you and watch over you.

PSALM 32:8 NIV

"Now then go, and I, even I, will be with your mouth, and teach you what you are to say."

EXODUS 4:12 NASB

PRAYERS

"Teach me, and I will be quiet; show me where I have been wrong."

JOB 6:24 NIV

Show me your ways, O Lord, teach me your paths; guide me in your truth and teach me, for you are God my Savior, and my hope is in you all day long. He guides the humble in what is right and teaches them his way.

PSALM 25:4,5,9 NIV

INSTRUCTIONS FOR YOUR CHILD

"Don't sin by letting anger gain control over you." Don't let the sun go down while you are still angry, for anger gives a mighty foothold to the Devil.... And do not bring sorrow to God's Holy Spirit by the way you live.... Be kind to each other, tenderhearted, forgiving one another, just as God through Christ has forgiven you.

EPHESIANS 4:26,27,30,32 NLT

In everything, therefore, treat people the same way you want them to treat you.

MATTHEW 7:12 NASB

God blesses those people who are merciful. They will be treated with mercy!

MATTHEW 5:7 CEV

EXAMPLES

The older brother of the Prodigal Son is a classic example of an offended son. The father listened, then quietly affirmed his love and concern:

"Look, dear son, you and I are very close, and everything I have is yours. We had to celebrate this happy day. For your brother was dead and has come back to life! He was lost, but now he is found."

LUKE 15:31,32 NLT

When believers withdraw from Jesus, He offers His fellowship and waits patiently for the door to open.

"Look! Here I stand at the door and knock. If you hear me calling and open the door, I will come in, and we will share a meal as friends. I will invite everyone who is victorious to sit with me on my throne."

REVELATION 3:20,21 NLT

Q: WHAT ARE SOME WAYS I
CAN ENCOURAGE MY CHILD?

A: Gently encourage the stragglers, and reach out for the exhausted, pulling them to their feet. Be patient with each person, attentive to individual needs.... Look for the best in each other, and always do your best to bring it out.

1 THESSALONIANS 5:14,15 THE MESSAGE

INSTRUCTIONS

Say only what helps, each word a gift.

EPHESIANS 4:29 THE MESSAGE

Share each other's troubles and problems, and in this way obey the law of Christ.

GALATIANS 6:2 NLT

Love...is ever ready to believe the best of every person, its hopes are fadeless under all circumstances.

1 CORINTHIANS 13:7 AMP

Never stop praying.... Always pray by the power of the Spirit.

EPHESIANS 6:18 CEV

PROMISES

The Lord God has given me his words of wisdom so that I may know what I should say to all these weary ones. Morning by morning he wakens me and opens my understanding to his will.

ISAIAH 50:4 TLB

All praise to the God and Father of our Lord Jesus Christ. He is the source of every mercy and the God who comforts us. He comforts us in all our troubles so that we can comfort others. When others are troubled, we will be able to give them the same comfort God has given us.

2 CORINTHIANS 1:3,4 NLT

TO PRAY FOR YOUR CHILD

May the God of hope fill you with all joy and peace as you trust in him, so that you may overflow with hope by the power of the Holy Spirit.

ROMANS 15:13 NIV

We pray for God's power to help you do all the good things that you hope to do and that your faith makes you want to do. Then...you will bring honor to the name of our Lord Jesus, and he will bring honor to you.

2 Thessalonians 1:11,12 CEV

Instructions for Your child

Happy is the person who doesn't listen to the wicked. He doesn't go where sinners go. He doesn't do what bad people do. He loves the Lord's teachings. He thinks about those teachings day and night. He is strong, like a tree planted by a river. It produces fruit in season. Its leaves don't die. Everything he does will succeed.

Psalm 1:1-3 ICB

"Be strong and courageous. Do not be afraid or terrified because of them, for the Lord your God goes with you; he will never leave you nor forsake you."

Deuteronomy 31:6 NIV

"Ask, and it will be given to you; seek, and you will find; knock, and it will be opened to you. For everyone who asks receives, and he who seeks finds, and to him who knocks it will be opened."

MATTHEW 7:7,8 NKJV

Give all your worries to him, because he cares for you.

1 PETER 5:7 ICB

The Lord is faithful, and He will strengthen and protect you from the evil one.

2 THESSALONIANS 3:3 NASB

You are from God, little children, and have overcome them; because greater is He who is in you than he who is in the world.

1 JOHN 4:4 NASB

I can do everything with the help of Christ who gives me the strength I need.

PHILIPPIANS 4:13 NLT

"For I, the Lord your God, will hold your right hand, saying to you, 'Fear not, I will help you.'"

ISAIAH 41:13 NKJV

The only temptations that you have are the temptations that all people have. But you can trust God. He will not let you be tempted more than you can stand. But when you are tempted, God will also give you a way to escape that temptation. Then you will be able to stand it.

1 CORINTHIANS 10:13 ICB

God began doing a good work in you. And he will continue it until it is finished when Jesus Christ comes again. I am sure of that.

PHILIPPIANS 1:6 ICB

EXAMPLE

Barnabas encouraged Saul when nobody else wanted to give him a chance:

When he [Saul] came to Jerusalem, he tried to join the disciples, but they were all afraid of him, not believing that he really was a disciple. But Barnabas took him and brought him to the apostles. He told them how Saul on his journey had seen the Lord and that the Lord had spoken to him, and how in Damascus he had preached fearlessly in the name of Jesus. So Saul stayed with them and moved about freely in Jerusalem, speaking boldly in the name of the Lord.

ACTS 9:26-28 NIV

Q: ABOVE ALL, I WANT TO BE
SURE MY CHILD KNOWS YOU,
LORD. WHAT SHOULD I DO?

A: Everywhere we go we talk about Christ
to all who will listen, warning them and teaching them as well as we know how. We want to
be able to present each one to God, perfect
because of what Christ has done for each of
them.

COLOSSIANS 1:28 TLB

To this end I labor, struggling with all his
energy, which so powerfully works in me.

COLOSSIANS 1:29 NIV

INSTRUCTIONS

Memorize these laws and think about them....
Teach them to your children. Talk about them
all the time — whether you're at home or
walking along the road or going to bed at
night, or getting up in the morning.

DEUTERONOMY 11:18,19 CEV

If anybody asks why believe as you do, be ready to tell him.

1 Peter 3:15 TLB

When you are with unbelievers, always make good use of the time. Be pleasant and hold their interest when you speak the message. Choose your words carefully and be ready to give answers to anyone who asks questions.

Colossians 4:5,6 CEV

Such confidence as this is ours through Christ before God. Not that we are competent in ourselves...but our competence comes from God. He has made us competent as ministers of a new covenant.

2 Corinthians 3:4-6 NIV

PROMISES

They said, "Believe on the Lord Jesus Christ, and you will be saved, you and your household."

Acts 16:31 NKJV

"I was found by those who did not seek me; I revealed myself to those who did not ask for me."

Romans 10:20 NIV

TO PRAY FOR YOUR CHILD

I...do not cease giving thanks for you, while making mention of you in my prayers; that the God of our Lord Jesus Christ, the Father of glory, may give to you a spirit of wisdom and of revelation in the knowledge of Him. I pray that the eyes of your heart may be enlightened, so that you will know what is the hope of His calling, what are the riches of the glory of His inheritance in the saints, and what is the sur-passing greatness of His power toward us who believe.

EPHESIANS 1:15-19 NASB

My response is to get down on my knees before the Father.... I ask him to strengthen you by his Spirit — not a brute strength but a glorious inner strength — that Christ will live in you as you open the door and invite him in.

EPHESIANS 3:14,16,17 THE MESSAGE

INSTRUCTIONS FOR YOUR CHILD

God loved the people of this world so much that he gave his only Son, so that everyone who has faith in him will have eternal life and never really die.

JOHN 3:16 CEV

If we say we have no sin, we are only fooling ourselves and refusing to accept the truth.

1 JOHN 1:8 NLT

But God demonstrates his own love for us in this: While we were still sinners, Christ died for us.

ROMANS 5:8 NIV

He was wounded and crushed for our sins. He was beaten that we might have peace. He was whipped, and we were healed! All of us have strayed away like sheep. We have left God's paths to follow our own. Yet the Lord laid on him the guilt and sins of us all.

ISAIAH 53:5,6 NLT

Yes, when Christ died, he died to defeat the power of sin one time — enough for all time. He now has a new life, and his new life is with God. In the same way, you should see your-selves as being dead to the power of sin and alive with God through Christ Jesus.... Be like people who have died and now live. Offer the parts of your body to God to be used for doing good. Sin will not be your master.

ROMANS 6:10,11,13,14 ICB

How can a young man stay pure? By reading your Word and following its rules. I have thought much about your words, and stored them in my heart so that they would hold me back from sin.

PSALM 119:9,11 TLB

"If you love me, you will obey my commands."

JOHN 14:15 NCV

From childhood you have known the Holy Scriptures, which are able to make you wise for salvation through faith which is in Christ Jesus.

2 TIMOTHY 3:15 NKJV

FOR YOUR CHILD TO PRAY

If you confess with your mouth that Jesus is Lord and believe in your heart that God raised him from the dead, you will be saved.

ROMANS 10:9 NLT

Take away my sin, and I will be clean. Wash me, and I will be whiter than snow.

PSALM 51:7 ICB

Blessed Lord, teach me your rules. I will meditate upon them and give them my full respect. I will delight in them and not forget them. Open my eyes to see wonderful things in your Word.

PSALM 119:12,15,16,18 TLB

PROMISES FOR YOUR CHILD

If anyone is in Christ, he is a new creation; old things have passed away; behold, all things have become new.

2 CORINTHIANS 5:17 NKJV

If we confess our sins to him, he is faithful and just to forgive us and to cleanse us from every wrong.

1 JOHN 1:9 NLT

The Lord your God will always be at your side, and he will never abandon you.

DEUTERONOMY 31:6 CEV

God is working in you to make you willing and able to obey him.

PHILIPPIANS 2:13 CEV

Be faithful until death, and I will give you the crown of life.

REVELATION 2:10 NASB

Q: HOW CAN I HELP MY
CHILDREN REACH THEIR
FULL POTENTIAL?

A: "It's not possible for a person to succeed
— I'm talking about eternal success — without
heaven's help."

JOHN 3:27 THE MESSAGE

Unless the Lord builds the house, they labor
in vain who build it; unless the Lord guards
the city, the watchman keeps awake in vain.

PSALM 127:1 NASB

O Lord my God...Your plans for us are too
numerous to list. If I tried to recite all your
wonderful deeds, I would never come to the
end of them.

PSALM 40:5 NLT

INSTRUCTIONS

We are fellow workmen — joint promoters,
laborers together — with and for God.

1 CORINTHIANS 3:9 AMP

Devote yourselves to prayer with an alert mind and a thankful heart.

COLOSSIANS 4:2 NLT

Be an example...with your words, your actions, your love, your faith, and your pure life. Continue to read the Scriptures to the people, strengthen them, and teach them. Be careful in your life and in your teaching. If you continue to live and teach rightly, you will save both yourself and those who listen to you.

1 TIMOTHY 4:12,13,16 NCV

TO PRAY FOR YOUR CHILD

I pray for good fortune in everything you do, and for your good health — that your everyday affairs prosper, as well as your soul!

3 JOHN 2 THE MESSAGE

We pray for God's power to help you do all the good things that you hope to do and that your faith makes you want to do. Then...you will bring honor to the name of our Lord Jesus, and he will bring honor to you.

2 THESSALONIANS 1:11,12 CEV

May the God of peace...equip you with all you need for doing his will. May he produce in you, through the power of Jesus Christ, all that is pleasing to him.

HEBREWS 13:20,21 NLT

INSTRUCTIONS FOR YOUR CHILD

You're blessed when you stay on course, walking steadily on the road revealed by God. You're blessed when you follow his directions, doing your best to find him. That's right — you don't go off on your own; you walk straight along the road he set.

PSALM 119:1-3 THE MESSAGE

"This book of the law shall not depart from your mouth, but you shall meditate on it day and night, so that you may be careful to do according to all that is written in it; for then you will make your way prosperous, and then you will have success."

JOSHUA 1:8 NASB

"Be strong and do not give up, for your work will be rewarded."

2 CHRONICLES 15:7 NIV

The lazy person will not get what he wants.

But a hard worker gets everything he wants.

PROVERBS 13:4 ICB

Refuse good advice and watch your plans fail; take good counsel and watch them succeed.

PROVERBS 15:22 THE MESSAGE

Form your purpose by asking for counsel, then carry it out using all the help you can get.

PROVERBS 20:18 THE MESSAGE

Do you see a man skilled in his work? That man will work for kings. He won't have to work for ordinary people.

PROVERBS 22:29 ICB

A lazy life is an empty life.

PROVERBS 12:27 THE MESSAGE

"Whoever wants to be great must become a servant."

MATTHEW 20:26 THE MESSAGE

PROMISES FOR YOUR CHILD

"For I know the plans I have for you," declares the Lord, "plans to prosper you and not to harm you, plans to give you hope and a future. Then you will call upon me and come and pray to me, and I will listen to you. You will seek me and find me when you seek me with all your heart."

JEREMIAH 29:11-13 NIV

God can pour on the blessings in astonishing ways so that you're ready for anything and everything.

2 CORINTHIANS 9:8 THE MESSAGE

I can do all things through Christ, because he gives me strength.

PHILIPPIANS 4:13 NCV

We are God's workmanship, created in Christ Jesus to do good works, which God prepared in advance for us to do.

EPHESIANS 2:10 NIV

EXAMPLE

King David encouraged his son Solomon as he worked to fulfill God's plan for his life.

"Be strong and courageous, and do the work. Do not be afraid or discouraged, for the Lord God, my God, is with you. He will not fail you or forsake you until all the work for the service of the temple of the Lord is finished.

1 CHRONICLES 28:20 NIV

———◈———

Q: GOD, IS THERE ANY WAY
I CAN HELP MY CHILD PICK
WHOLESOME FRIENDS?

———◈———

A: We warn them and teach them with all
the wisdom God has given us, for we want to
present them to God, perfect in their relationship to Christ. I work very hard at this, as I
depend on Christ's mighty power that works
within me.

COLOSSIANS 1:28,29 NLT

PROMISES

He who fears the Lord has a secure fortress,
and for his children it will be a refuge.

PROVERBS 14:26 NIV

The Lord grants wisdom! His every word is a
treasure of knowledge and understanding. He
grants good sense to the godly — his saints.
He is their shield, protecting them and guard-
ing their pathway. He shows how to distin-
guish right from wrong, how to find the right

decision every time.

PROVERBS 2:6-9 TLB

The Lord...will bring to light what is hidden in darkness and will expose the motives of men's hearts.

1 CORINTHIANS 4:5 NIV

TO PRAY FOR YOUR CHILD

For wisdom will enter your heart, and knowledge will be pleasant to your soul; discretion will guard you, understanding will watch over you, to deliver you from the way of evil, from the man who speaks perverse things; from those who leave the paths of uprightness, to walk in the ways of darkness.... Whose paths are crooked, and who are devious in their ways.... So you will walk in the way of good men and keep to the paths of the righteous.

PROVERBS 2:10-13,15,20 NASB

INSTRUCTIONS FOR YOUR CHILD

Pursue faith and love and peace, and enjoy the companionship of those who call on the Lord with pure hearts.

2 TIMOTHY 2:22 NLT

I am a friend to everyone who fears you. I am a friend to anyone who follows your orders.

PSALM 119:63 ICB

Whoever spends time with wise people will become wise. But whoever makes friends with fools will suffer.

PROVERBS 13:20 ICB

Stay away from a foolish person. You won't learn anything from him. What makes a person wise is understanding what to do. But what makes a person foolish is dishonesty. Foolish people don't care if they sin. But honest people work at being right with others.

PROVERBS 14:7-9 ICB

Friends come and friends go, but a true friend sticks by you like family

PROVERBS 18:24 THE MESSAGE

Don't make friends with someone who easily gets angry. Don't spend time with someone who has a bad temper. If you do, you may learn to be like him. Then you will be in real danger.

PROVERBS 22:24,25 ICB

You must not associate with...anyone who calls

himself a brother in Christ but who takes part in sexual sin, or is selfish, or worships idols, or lies about others, or gets drunk, or cheats people. Do not even eat with someone like that.

1 CORINTHIANS 5:11 ICB

Do not be fooled: "Bad friends will ruin good habits."

1 CORINTHIANS 15:33 NCV

Don't team up with those who are unbelievers. How can goodness be a partner with wickedness? How can light live with darkness? What harmony can there be between Christ and the Devil? How can a believer be a partner with an unbeliever? As God said: "I will live in them and walk among them. I will be their God, and they will be my people. Therefore, come out from them and separate yourselves from them, says the Lord. Don't touch their filthy things, and I will welcome you."

2 CORINTHIANS 6:14-17 NLT

PROMISES FOR YOUR CHILD

Happy is the person who doesn't listen to the wicked. He doesn't go where sinners go. He doesn't do what bad people do. He loves the

Lord's teachings. He thinks about those teachings day and night. He is strong, like a tree planted by a river. It produces fruit in season. Its leaves don't die. Everything he does will succeed.

PSALM 1:1-3 ICB

You have known the Holy Scriptures since you were a child. The Scriptures are able to make you wise.

2 TIMOTHY 3:15 ICB

For wisdom and truth will enter the very center of your being, filling your life with joy. You will be given the sense to stay away from evil men.

PROVERBS 2:10,11 TLB

EXAMPLE

The Lord declared He would put a "hedge of protection" around Gomer to cut her off from evil friends:

"I will block her road with thornbushes. I will build a wall around her so she cannot find her way. She will run after her lovers. But she won't catch up to them. She will look for them. But she won't find them."

HOSEA 2:6,7 ICB

Q: HOW CAN I HELP MY
CHILDREN WITH PEER PRESSURE
AND TEACH THEM TO STAND
ALONE WHEN NECESSARY?

A: Train up a child in the way he should go,
even when he is old he will not depart from it.

PROVERBS 22:6 NASB

INSTRUCTIONS

Speak up for the right living that goes along
with true Christianity.... Urge the young men
to behave carefully, taking life seriously. And
here you yourself must be an example to them
of good deeds of every kind. Let everything
you do reflect your love of the truth and the
fact that you are in dead earnest about it.

TITUS 2:1,6,7 TLB

PROMISES

"The Lord who made you and helps you

says...my chosen one, do not fear....I will pour out my Spirit and my blessings on your children. They will thrive like watered grass, like willows on a riverbank. Some will proudly claim, 'I belong to the Lord.' Others will say, 'I am a descendant of Jacob.' Some will write the Lord's name on their hands and will take the honored name of Israel as their own.

ISAIAH 44:2-5 NLT

To Pray for Your Child

"For this boy I prayed, and the Lord has given me my petition which I asked of Him.
"So I have also dedicated him to the Lord; as long as he lives he is dedicated to the Lord."

1 SAMUEL 1:27,28 NASB

I have given them your word. And the world hates them because they do not belong to the world, just as I do not. I'm not asking you to take them out of the world, but to keep them safe from the evil one. They are not part of this world any more than I am. Make them pure and holy by teaching them your words of truth. As you sent me into the world, I am sending them into the world. And I give myself entirely to you so they also might be entirely yours.

JOHN 17:14-19 NLT

May the God of peace himself make you entirely pure and devoted to God; and may your spirit and soul and body be kept strong and blameless until that day when our Lord Jesus Christ comes back again.

1 THESSALONIANS 5:23 TLB

INSTRUCTIONS FOR YOUR CHILD

Ask the Lord Jesus Christ to help you live as you should, and don't make plans to enjoy evil.

ROMANS 13:14 TLB

"Do not follow the crowd in doing wrong."

EXODUS 23:2 NIV

Don't sin because others do, but stay close to God.

1 TIMOTHY 5:22 CEV

Keep yourself pure.

1 TIMOTHY 5:22 NKJV

Put on the full armor of God, so that when the day of evil comes, you may be able to stand your ground.

EPHESIANS 6:13 NIV

Run from temptations that capture young people. Always do the right thing.

2 TIMOTHY 2:22 CEV

The common bond of rebels is their guilt. The common bond of godly people is good will.

PROVERBS 14:9 TLB

Don't follow the ways of the wicked. Don't do what evil people do. Avoid their ways. Don't go near what they do. Stay away from them and keep on going. They cannot sleep until they do evil. They cannot rest until they hurt someone. They fill themselves with wickedness and cruelty as if they were eating bread and drinking wine. The way of the good person is like the light of dawn. It grows brighter and brighter until it is full daylight. But the wicked are like those who stumble in the dark. They can't even see what has hurt them.

PROVERBS 4:14-19 ICB

If young toughs tell you, "Come and join us" — turn your back on them! "We'll hide and rob and kill," they say. "Good or bad, we'll treat them all alike. And the loot we'll get! All kinds of stuff! Come on, throw in your lot with us;

we'll split with you in equal shares."

Don't do it, son! Stay far from men like that, for crime is their way of life, and murder is their specialty. They will die a violent death.

PROVERBS 1:10-16,19 TLB

God blesses those people who are treated badly for doing right. They belong to the kingdom of heaven. God will bless you when people insult you, mistreat you, and tell all kinds of evil lies about you because of me. Be happy and excited! You will have a great reward in heaven. People did these same things to the prophets who lived long ago.

MATTHEW 5:10-12 CEV

FOR YOUR CHILD TO PRAY

How can a young person live a pure life? He can do it by obeying your word. With all my heart I try to obey you, God. Don't let me break your commands. I have taken your words to heart so I would not sin against you. Lord, you should be praised. Teach me your demands.

PSALM 119:9-12 ICB

Lord, defend me. I have lived an innocent life. I trusted the Lord and never doubted. Lord, try me and test me. Look closely into my heart and mind. I see your love. I live by your truth. I do not spend time with liars. I do not make friends with people who hide their sin. I hate the company of evil people. I have lived an innocent life. So save me and be kind to me.

PSALM 26:1-5,11 ICB

The Lord is my light and my salvation; whom shall I fear? The Lord is the strength of my life; of whom shall I be afraid?

PSALM 27:1 NKJV

If God is for us, who can be against us?

ROMANS 8:31 NKJV

EXAMPLES

Shadrach, Meshach, and Abednego stood together against tremendous pressure. Because they stead-fastly refused to bow down and worship the golden idol, God protected and promoted them:

The fire hadn't touched them — not a hair of

their heads was singed; their coats were unscorched, and they didn't even smell of smoke! Then Nebuchadnezzar said, "Blessed be the God of Shadrach, Meshach, and Abednego, for he sent his angel to deliver his trusting servants when they defied the king's commandment and were willing to die rather than serve or worship any god except their own." Then the king gave promotions to Shadrach, Meshach, and Abednego, so that they prospered greatly there in the province of Babylon.

DANIEL 3:27,28,30 TLB

Moses also chose to side with God instead of with the people around him:

By faith Moses, when he had grown up, refused to be known as the son of Pharaoh's daughter. He chose to be mistreated along with the people of God rather than to enjoy the pleasures of sin for a short time.

HEBREWS 11:24,25 NIV

Because of his faith, Moses left Egypt. Moses had seen the invisible God and wasn't afraid of the king's anger.

HEBREWS 11:27 CEV

Q: How can I teach my child the value of honesty?

A: Be an example...with your words, your actions, your love, your faith, and your pure life.

1 Timothy 4:12 NCV

We have always lived honestly and sincerely, especially when we were with you. And we were guided by God's wonderful kindness instead of by the wisdom of this world.... God can be trusted, and so can I.

2 Corinthians 1:12,18 CEV

Instructions

Be careful, and watch yourselves closely so that you do not forget the things your eyes have seen or let them slip from your heart as long as you live. Teach them to your children and to their children after them.

Deuteronomy 4:9 NIV

God-loyal people, living honest lives, make it much easier for their children.

PROVERBS 20:7 THE MESSAGE

All your sons will be taught by the Lord, and great will be your children's peace.

ISAIAH 54:13 NIV

TO PRAY FOR YOUR CHILD

We have continued praying for you, asking God that you will know fully what he wants. We pray that you will also have great wisdom and understanding in spiritual things so that you will live the kind of life that honors and pleases the Lord in every way.... God has freed us from the power of darkness, and he brought us into the kingdom of his dear Son.

COLOSSIANS 1:9,10,13 NCV

INSTRUCTIONS FOR YOUR CHILD

Lovingly follow the truth at all times — speaking truly, dealing truly, living truly — and so become more and more in every way like Christ.

EPHESIANS 4:15 TLB

Tell your neighbor the truth....When you lie to others, you end up lying to yourself.

EPHESIANS 4:25 THE MESSAGE

An honest life shows respect for God; a degenerate life is a slap in his face.

PROVERBS 14:2 THE MESSAGE

Don't use your mouth to tell lies. Don't ever say things that are not true.

PROVERBS 4:24 ICB

Stop lying to each other. You have given up your old way of life with its habits. Each of you is now a new person. You are becoming more and more like your Creator.

COLOSSIANS 3:9,10 CEV

Truth will last forever. But lies last only a moment.

PROVERBS 12:19 ICB

The person who tells lies gets caught; the person who spreads rumors is ruined.

PROVERBS 19:9 THE MESSAGE

Good people will be guided by honesty. But dishonesty will destroy those who are not trustworthy.

PROVERBS 11:3 ICB

These liars have lied so well and for so long that they've lost their capacity for truth.

1 TIMOTHY 4:2 THE MESSAGE

PROMISES FOR YOUR CHILD

Do any of you want to live a life that is long and good? Then watch your tongue! Keep your lips from telling lies! Turn away from evil and do good. Work hard at living in peace with others. The eyes of the Lord watch over those who do right; his ears are open to their cries for help. But the Lord turns his face against those who do evil; he will erase their memory from the earth. The Lord hears his people when they call to him for help. He rescues them from all their troubles...from each and every one.

PSALM 34:12-17,19 NLT

If anyone is in Christ, he is a new creation; old things have passed away; behold, all things have become new.

2 CORINTHIANS 5:17 NKJV

God is working in you to make you willing and able to obey him.

PHILIPPIANS 2:13 CEV

FOR YOUR CHILD TO PRAY

You deserve honesty from the heart; yes, utter sincerity and truthfulness.... Create in me a new, clean heart, O God, filled with clean thoughts and right desires.

PSALM 51:6,10 TLB

You want me to be completely truthful. So teach me wisdom. Take away my sin, and I will be clean. Wash me, and I will be whiter than snow.

PSALM 51:6,7 ICB

EXAMPLES

There are many accounts in the Bible of people telling lies. Notice how each of these lies brought consequences:

Then Peter began to curse. He said, "May a curse fall on me if I'm not telling the truth. I don't know the man." After Peter said this, a rooster crowed. Then he remembered what Jesus had told him: "Before the rooster crows, you will say three times that you don't know me." Then Peter went outside and cried painfully.

MATTHEW 26:74,75 ICB

Now he went in and stood before his master. Elisha said to him, "Where did you go, Gehazi?" And he said, "Your servant did not go anywhere." Then he said to him, "Did not my heart go with you when the man turned back from his chariot to meet you? Is it time to receive money and to receive clothing, olive groves and vineyards, sheep and oxen, male and female servants? Therefore the leprosy of Naaman shall cling to you and your descendants forever." And he went out from his presence leprous, as white as snow.

2 KINGS 5:25-27 NKJV

Now it was about three hours later when his wife came in, not knowing what had happened. And Peter answered her, "Tell me whether you sold the land for so much?" She said, "Yes, for so much." Then Peter said to her, "How is it that you have agreed together to test the Spirit of the Lord? Look, the feet of those who have buried your husband are at the door, and they will carry you out." Then immediately she fell down at his feet and breathed her last.

ACTS 5:7-10 NKJV

Q: WHAT CAN I DO ABOUT SIBLING RIVALRY? IS THERE A WAY TO STOP STRIFE IN MY HOME?

A: Promote the kind of living that reflects right teaching.... Encourage the young men to live wisely in all they do. And you yourself must be an example to them by doing good deeds of every kind. Let everything you do reflect the integrity and seriousness of your teaching.

TITUS 2:1,6-8 NLT

INSTRUCTIONS

The servant of the Lord must not be quarrelsome — fighting and contending. Instead he must be kindly to every one and mild-tempered — preserving the bond of peace.

2 TIMOTHY 2:24 AMP

Submit to one another out of reverence for Christ. Wives, submit to your husbands as to the Lord. Husbands, love your wives, just as

Christ loved the church. Children, obey your parents in the Lord, for this is right.

EPHESIANS 5:21,22,25;6:1 NIV

Don't show favouritism.

JAMES 2:1 NIV

PROMISES

Correct your son, and he will give you rest; yes, he will give delight to your heart.

PROVERBS 29:17 AMP

All your...children shall be disciples — taught of the Lord [and obedient to His will]; and great shall be the peace and undisturbed composure of your children.

ISAIAH 54:13 AMP

It is written in the book of the prophets, And they shall all be taught of God — have Him in person for their teacher.

JOHN 6:45 AMP

TO PRAY FOR YOUR CHILD

I pray that God will be kind to you and will let you live in perfect peace! May you keep learning more and more about God and our

Lord Jesus.... Do your best to improve your faith. You can do this by adding goodness, understanding, self-control, patience, devotion to God, concern for others, and love. If you keep growing in this way, it will show that what you know about our Lord Jesus Christ has made your lives useful and meaningful.

2 PETER 1:2,5-8 CEV

Now the God of peace...Make you perfect in every good work to do his will, working in you that which is wellpleasing in his sight, through Jesus Christ.

HEBREWS 13:20,21 KJV

INSTRUCTIONS FOR YOUR CHILD

Always be willing to listen and slow to speak. Do not become angry easily.

JAMES 1:19 ICB

When you do things, do not let selfishness or pride be your guide. Instead, be humble and give more honor to others than to yourselves. Do not be interested only in your own life, but be interested in the lives of others.

PHILIPPIANS 2:3,4 NCV

"Here is a simple, rule-of-thumb guide for

behavior: Ask yourself what you want people to do for you, then grab the initiative and do it for them."

MATTHEW 7:12 THE MESSAGE

Don't use bad language. Say only what is good and helpful to those you are talking to, and what will give them a blessing.

EPHESIANS 4:29 TLB

A gentle answer will calm a person's anger. But an unkind answer will cause more anger.

PROVERBS 15:1 ICB

Get rid of all bitterness, rage and anger, brawling and slander, along with every form of malice. Be kind and compassionate to one another, forgiving each other, just as in Christ God forgave you. Be imitators of God, therefore, as dearly loved children and live a life of love.

EPHESIANS 4:31-5:2 NIV

For the whole law can be summed up in this one command: "Love your neighbor as yourself." But if instead of showing love among yourselves you are always biting and devouring one another, watch out! Beware of destroying one another.

GALATIANS 5:14,15 NLT

Do you know where your fights and arguments come from? They come from the selfish desires that make war inside you. You want things, but you do not have them. So you are ready to kill and are jealous of other people. But you still cannot get what you want. So you argue and fight. You do not get what you want because you do not ask God.

JAMES 4:1,2 ICB

Let the peace of Christ keep you in tune with each other, in step with each other. None of this going off and doing your own thing. And cultivate thankfulness.

COLOSSIANS 3:15 THE MESSAGE

Do not do wrong to a person to pay him back for doing wrong to you. Or do not insult someone to pay him back for insulting you. But ask God to bless that person. Do this, because you yourselves were called to receive a blessing.... If you are always trying to do good, no one can really hurt you.

1 PETER 3:9,13 ICB

PROMISES FOR YOUR CHILD

When a man's ways are pleasing to the Lord,

He makes even his enemies to be at peace with him.

PROVERBS 16:7 NASB

Those who are peacemakers will plant seeds of peace and reap a harvest of goodness.

JAMES 3:18 NLT

Work hard at living in peace with others. The eyes of the Lord watch over those who do right, and his ears are open to their prayers. But the Lord turns his face against those who do evil.

1 PETER 3:11,12 NLT

FOR YOUR CHILD TO PRAY

"Love your enemies. Pray for those who hurt you. If you do this, then you will be true sons of your Father in heaven."

MATTHEW 5:44,45 ICB

Here are some examples of that type of prayer:

Jesus said, "Father, forgive them. They don't know what they are doing."

LUKE 23:34 ICB

He [Stephen] fell on his knees and cried out, "Lord, do not hold this sin against them."

ACTS 7:60 NIV

EXAMPLES

Beware of showing favoritism to your children. Tremendous damage to a family can result:

So Esau bore a grudge against Jacob because of the blessing with which his father had blessed him; and Esau said to himself, "The days of mourning for my father are near; then I will kill my brother Jacob."

GENESIS 27:41 NASB

Now as it happened, Israel loved Joseph more than any of his other children, because Joseph was born to him in his old age. So one day Jacob gave him a special gift — a brightly-colored coat. His brothers of course noticed their father's partiality, and consequently hated Joseph; they couldn't say a kind word to him.

GENESIS 37:3,4 TLB

Q: HELP, LORD! MY CHILD IS SICK. WHAT SHOULD I DO?

A: He who fears the Lord has a secure fortress, and for his children it will be a refuge.

PROVERBS 14:26 NIV

The Lord says, "I will rescue those who love me. I will protect those who trust in my name. When they call on me, I will answer; I will be with them in trouble. I will rescue them and honor them. I will satisfy them with a long life and give them my salvation."

PSALM 91:14-16 NLT

INSTRUCTIONS

Is any one of you sick? He should call the elders of the church to pray over him and anoint him with oil in the name of the Lord. And the prayer offered in faith will make the sick person well; the Lord will raise him up. If he has sinned, he will be forgiven. Therefore confess your sins to each other and pray for each other so that you may be healed. The prayer of a righteous man is powerful and effective.

JAMES 5:14-16 NIV

"These signs will follow those who believe: In My name they will cast out demons...they will lay hands on the sick, and they will recover."

MARK 16:17,18 NKJV

They will touch the sick, and the sick will be healed.

MARK 16:18 NCV

The truth is, anyone who believes in me will do the same works I have done, and even greater works, because I am going to be with the Father. You can ask for anything in my name, and I will do it, because the work of the Son brings glory to the Father.

JOHN 14:12,13 NLT

God's love, though, is ever and always, eternally present to all who fear him, making everything right for them and their children as they follow his Covenant ways and remember to do whatever he said.

PSALM 103:17,18 THE MESSAGE

Seek the Lord and His strength; seek His face

evermore! Remember His marvelous works which He has done, His wonders, and the judgments of His mouth. He remembers His covenant forever, the word which He commanded, for a thousand generations.

PSALM 105:4,5,8 NKJV

Never give up praying. And when you pray, keep alert and be thankful.

COLOSSIANS 4:2 CEV

Give thanks to the Lord and proclaim his greatness. Let the whole world know what he has done. Sing to him; yes, sing his praises. Tell everyone about his miracles.... O worshipers of the Lord, rejoice!

PSALM 105:1-3 NLT

Oh my soul, bless God, don't forget a single blessing! He forgives your sins — every one. He heals your diseases — every one.

PSALM 103:2,3 THE MESSAGE

What shall I render to the Lord for all His benefits toward me? I will take up the cup of salvation, and call upon the name of the Lord. I will offer to You the sacrifice of thanksgiving, and will call upon the name of the Lord.

PSALM 116:12,13,17 NKJV

PROMISES

Of all the people on earth, the Lord your God has chosen you to be his own special treasure... He is the faithful God who keeps his covenant for a thousand generations and constantly loves those who love him and obey his commands. He will love you and bless you.... And the Lord will protect you from all sickness.

DEUTERONOMY 7:6,9,13,15 NLT

Our children too shall serve him, for they shall hear from us about the wonders of the Lord; generations yet unborn shall hear of all the miracles he did for us.

PSALM 22:30,31 TLB

He sent forth his word and healed them; he rescued them from the grave.

PSALM 107:20 NIV

"Be strong and of good courage, do not fear nor be afraid of them; for the Lord your God, He is the One who goes with you. He will not leave you nor forsake you."

DEUTERONOMY 31:6 NKJV

TO PRAY FOR YOUR CHILD

I pray that God, who gives peace, will make you completely holy. And may your spirit, soul, and body be kept healthy and faultless until our Lord Jesus returns. The one who chose you can be trusted, and he will do this.

1 THESSALONIANS 5:23,24 CEV

He is my God, and I am trusting him. For he rescues you from every trap, and protects you from the fatal plague. He will shield you with his wings! They will shelter you. His faithful promises are your armor.

PSALM 91:2-4 TLB

In your day of trouble, may the Lord be with you! May the God of Jacob keep you from all harm. May there be shouts of joy when we hear the news of your victory, flags flying with praise to God for all that he has done for you.

PSALM 20:1,5 TLB

"Whatever you ask for in prayer, believe that you have received it, and it will be yours."

MARK 11:24 NIV

INSTRUCTIONS FOR YOUR CHILD

Pay attention, my child, to what I say. Listen carefully. Don't lose sight of my words. Let them penetrate deep within your heart, for they bring life and radiant health to anyone who discovers their meaning.

PROVERBS 4:20-22 NLT

Trust in the Lord with all your heart and do not lean on your own understanding. In all your ways acknowledge Him, and He will make your paths straight. Do not be wise in your own eyes; fear the Lord and turn away from evil. It will be healing to your body and refreshment to your bones.

PROVERBS 3:5-8 NASB

PROMISES FOR YOUR CHILD

"I will restore you to health and heal your wounds," declares the Lord.

JEREMIAH 30:17 NIV

He took our suffering on him and felt our pain for us. We saw his suffering. We thought God was punishing him. But he was wounded for the wrong things we did. He was crushed for the evil things we did. The punishment, which made us well, was given to him. And we are healed because of his wounds.

ISAIAH 53:4,5 ICB

Christ carried our sins in his body on the cross. He did this so that we would stop living for sin and start living for what is right. And we are healed because of his wounds.

1 PETER 2:24 ICB

You must worship the Lord your God. If you do, I will bless your bread and your water. I will take away sickness from you. I will allow you to live long lives.

EXODUS 23:25,26 ICB

Jesus said to him, "I will go and heal him."

MATTHEW 8:7 NIV

Jesus Christ never changes! He is the same yesterday, today, and forever.

HEBREWS 13:8 CEV

FOR YOUR CHILD TO PRAY

Heal me, O Lord, and I will be healed; save me and I will be saved, for you are the one I praise.

JEREMIAH 17:14 NIV

My whole being, praise the Lord. Do not forget all his kindnesses. The Lord forgives me for all my sins. He heals all my diseases.

PSALM 103:2,3 ICB

Lord, how you have helped me before! You took me safely from my mother's womb and brought me through the years of infancy. I have depended upon you since birth; you have always been my God. Don't leave me now, for trouble is near and no one else can possibly help.

PSALM 22:9-11 TLB

EXAMPLES

There are many examples in the Bible of parents asking for — and receiving — healing for their children. Here are two:

Someone in the crowd shouted, "Teacher, please do something for my son! He is my only child." Jesus ordered the demon to stop. Then he healed the boy and gave him back to his father. Everyone was amazed at God's great power.

LUKE 9:38,42,43 CEV

Here is a great story of a mother's persistent faith:

A Gentile woman...came to him, pleading, "Have mercy on me, O Lord, Son of David! For my daughter has a demon in her, and it is severely tormenting her."

...He said to the woman, "I was sent only to help the people of Israel — God's lost sheep — not the Gentiles." But she came and worshiped him and pleaded again, "Lord, help me!"

"It isn't right to take food from the children and throw it to the dogs," he said.

"Yes, Lord," she replied, "but even dogs are permitted to eat crumbs that fall beneath their master's table."

"Woman," Jesus said to her, "your faith is great. Your request is granted." And her daughter was instantly healed.

MATTHEW 15:22,24-28 NLT

Keep on asking, and you will be given what you ask for. Keep on looking, and you will find. Keep on knocking, and the door will be opened. For everyone who asks, receives. Everyone who seeks, finds. And the door is opened to everyone who knocks.

MATTHEW 7:7,8 NLT

Q: How can I be sure my child is telling me the truth? I need discernment, Lord!

A: Ears to hear and eyes to see — both are gifts from the Lord.

PROVERBS 20:12 NLT

INSTRUCTIONS

"Call to me and I will answer you and tell you great and unsearchable things you do not know."

JEREMIAH 33:3 NIV

"There is nothing covered up that will not be revealed, and hidden that will not be known."

LUKE 12:2 NASB

The heart of the discerning acquires knowledge; the ears of the wise seek it out.

PROVERBS 18:15 NIV

Understanding a person's thoughts is as hard as getting water from a deep well. But someone with understanding can find the wisdom there.

PROVERBS 20:5 ICB

We know these things because God has revealed them to us by his Spirit, and his Spirit searches out everything. 1 CORINTHIANS 2:10 NLT

Trust in the Lord with all your heart and do not lean on your own understanding. In all your ways acknowledge Him, and He will make your paths straight. PROVERBS 3:5,6 NASB

Woe to those who go to great depths to hide their plans from the Lord, who do their work in darkness and think, "Who sees us? Who will know?" You turn things upside down, as if the potter were thought to be like the clay! Shall what is formed say to him who formed it, "He did not make me"? Can the pot say of the potter, "He knows nothing"? ISAIAH 29:15,16 NIV

"But when He, the Spirit of truth, comes, He will guide you into all the truth...He will disclose to you what is to come."

JOHN 16:13 NASB

He will bring to light what is hidden in darkness and will expose the motives of men's hearts.

1 CORINTHIANS 4:5 NIV

PRAYERS

Send forth your light and your truth, let them guide me.

PSALM 43:3 NIV

I will praise the Lord, who counsels me; even at night my heart instructs me. I have set the Lord always before me. Because he is at my right hand, I will not be shaken.

PSALM 16:7,8 NIV

EXAMPLE

When God revealed the king's dream to Daniel in a vision, the king fell on his face and said:

"Surely your God is the God of gods and the Lord of kings and a revealer of mysteries, for you were able to reveal this mystery."

DANIEL 2:47 NIV

Q: It's been a tough day, Lord. Do you have any words of encouragement for me?

A: "Do not fear, for I am with you; do not anxiously look about you, for I am your God. I will strengthen you, surely I will help you, surely I will uphold you with My righteous right hand."

ISAIAH 41:10 NASB

Whatever I have, wherever I am, I can make it through anything in the One who makes me who I am.

PHILIPPIANS 4:13 THE MESSAGE

INSTRUCTIONS

Cast your burden upon the Lord and He will sustain you; He will never allow the righteous to be shaken.

PSALM 55:22 NASB

Fix your thoughts on what is true and good and right. Think about things that are pure and lovely, and dwell on the fine, good things in others. Think about all you can praise God for and be glad about. Keep putting into practice all you learned from me...and the God of peace will be with you.

PHILIPPIANS 4:8,9 TLB

Let the peace of heart that comes from Christ be always present in your hearts and lives.... And always be thankful.

COLOSSIANS 3:15 TLB

Let us hold unswervingly to the hope we profess, for he who promised is faithful.

HEBREWS 10:23 NIV

Nothing you do for him is a waste of time or effort.

1 CORINTHIANS 15:58 THE MESSAGE

We fix our eyes not on what is seen, but on what is unseen. For what is seen is temporary, but what is unseen is eternal.

2 CORINTHIANS 4:18 NIV

We live by faith, not by sight.

2 CORINTHIANS 5:7 NIV

Now faith is being sure of what we hope for and certain of what we do not see.

HEBREWS 11:1 NIV

Even though on the outside it often looks like things are falling apart on us, on the inside, where God is making new life, not a day goes by without his unfolding grace.

2 CORINTHIANS 4:16 THE MESSAGE

We are like clay jars in which this treasure is stored. The real power comes from God and not from us. Even when we don't know what to do, we never give up. In times of trouble, God is with us, and when we are knocked down, we get up again.

2 CORINTHIANS 4:7-9 CEV

We felt like we'd been sent to death row, that it was all over for us. As it turned out, it was the best thing that could have happened. Instead of trusting in our own strength or wits to get out of it, we were forced to trust God totally — not a bad idea since he's the God who raises the dead!

2 CORINTHIANS 1:9 THE MESSAGE

PROMISES

And I am sure that God, who began the good work within you, will continue his work until it is finally finished on that day when Christ Jesus comes back again.

PHILIPPIANS 1:6 NLT

Be energetic in your life of salvation, reverent and sensitive before God. That energy is God's energy, an energy deep within you, God himself willing and working at what will give him the most pleasure.

PHILIPPIANS 2:12,13 THE MESSAGE

PRAYERS

We pray that you'll have the strength to stick it out over the long haul...strength that endures the unendurable and spills over into joy.

COLOSSIANS 1:11,12 THE MESSAGE

We wait in hope for the Lord; he is our help and our shield. In him our hearts rejoice, for we trust in his holy name. May your unfailing love rest upon us, O Lord, even as we put our hope in you.

PSALM 33:20-22 NIV

I wait for the Lord, my soul does wait, and in His word do I hope. My soul waits for the Lord more than the watchmen for the morning.... Hope in the Lord; for with the Lord there is lovingkindness, and with Him is abundant redemption.

PSALM 130:5-7 NASB

When You said, "Seek My face," my heart said to You, "Your face, O Lord, I shall seek." I would have despaired unless I had believed that I would see the goodness of the Lord in the land of the living.

PSALM 27:8,13 NASB

The minute I said, "I'm slipping, I'm falling," your love, God, took hold and held me fast. When I was upset and beside myself, you calmed me down and cheered me up.

PSALM 94:18,19 THE MESSAGE

Now to Him who is able to keep you from stumbling, and to make you stand in the presence of His glory blameless with great joy, to the only God our Savior, through Jesus Christ our Lord, be glory, majesty, dominion and authority.

JUDE 24,25 NASB

EXAMPLE

Recurring problems can be a "gift" — if they help us break the habit of relying on ourselves. Painfully aware of our own limitations, we turn towards

God's grace, receive His strength, and experience His peace in the midst of the storm.

Satan's angel did his best to get me down; what he in fact did was push me to my knees. No danger then of walking around high and mighty! At first I didn't think of it as a gift, and begged God to remove it. Three times I did that, and then he told me, "My grace is enough; it's all you need. My strength comes into its own in your weakness".... It was a case of Christ's strength moving in on my weakness. Now I take limitations in stride, and with good cheer.... I just let Christ take over! And so the weaker I get, the stronger I become.

2 CORINTHIANS 12:7-10 THE MESSAGE

He gives power to the faint and weary, and to him who has no might He increases strength — causing it to multiply and making it abound.

ISAIAH 40:29 AMP

—⟨∞⟩—

Q: MY CHILD HAS WALKED AWAY
FROM YOU, AND I FEAR THE
CONSEQUENCES OF THEIR
LIFESTYLE. WHAT NOW, LORD?

—⟨∞⟩—

A: I give you peace, the kind of peace that only I can give. It isn't like the peace that this world can give. So don't be worried or afraid.

JOHN 14:27 CEV

Who is among you who [reverently] fears the Lord, who obeys the voice of His servant, yet who walks in darkness and deep trouble and has no shining splendor [in his heart]? Let him rely on, trust and be confident in the name of the Lord, and let him lean upon and be supported by His God.

ISAIAH 50:10 AMP

For the Lord God helps me; therefore have I not been ashamed or confounded; therefore have I set my face like a flint, and I know that I shall not be put to shame.

ISAIAH 50:7 AMP

I would have despaired unless I had believed
that I would see the goodness of the Lord in
the land of the living. Wait for the Lord; be
strong and let your heart take courage; yes,
wait for the Lord.

PSALM 27:13,14 NASB

INSTRUCTIONS

Be an example to the believers with your
words, your actions, your love, your faith, and
your pure life.

1 TIMOTHY 4:12 NCV

Stay away from foolish and stupid arguments,
because you know they grow into quarrels. And
a servant of the Lord must not quarrel but
must be kind to everyone, a good teacher, and
patient. The Lord's servant must gently teach
those who disagree.

2 TIMOTHY 2:23-25 NCV

"Take into your heart all My words which I
will speak to you and listen closely. Go to...the
sons of your people, and speak to them and tell
them, whether they listen or not."

EZEKIEL 3:10,11 NASB

The god of this age has blinded the minds of

unbelievers, so that they cannot see the light of the gospel of the glory of Christ, who is the image of God.

2 CORINTHIANS 4:4 NIV

I urge, then, first of all, that requests, prayers, intercession and thanksgiving be made for everyone.... This is good, and pleases God our Savior, who wants all men to be saved and to come to a knowledge of the truth.

1 TIMOTHY 2:1,3,4 NIV

Pray without ceasing.

1 THESSALONIANS 5:17 NKJV

"To open their eyes so that they may turn from darkness to light and from the dominion of Satan to God, that they may receive forgiveness of sins and an inheritance among those who have been sanctified by faith in Me."

ACTS 26:18 NASB

Now this is the confidence that we have in Him, that if we ask anything according to His will, He hears us. And if we know that He hears us, whatever we ask, we know that we have the petitions that we have asked of Him.

1 JOHN 5:14,15 NKJV

"Behold, I have given you authority to tread on serpents and scorpions, and over all the power of the enemy, and nothing will injure you."

LUKE 10:19 NASB

"And I will give you the keys of the kingdom of heaven, and whatever you bind on earth will be bound in heaven, and whatever you loose on earth will be loosed in heaven."

MATTHEW 16:19 NKJV

To Pray for Your Child

I pray that the eyes of your heart may be enlightened.

EPHESIANS 1:18 NASB

We ask God to give you a complete understanding of what he wants to do in your lives, and we ask him to make you wise with spiritual wisdom.

COLOSSIANS 1:9 NLT

And may the God of peace Himself sanctify you through and through — that is, separate you from profane things, make you pure and wholly consecrated to God — and may your spirit and soul and body be preserved sound and complete [and found] blameless at the coming of our Lord Jesus Christ, the Messiah. Faithful is He Who is calling you [to Himself] and utterly trustworthy, and He will also do it [that is, fulfill His call by hallowing and keeping you].

1 THESSALONIANS 5:23,24 AMP

Now may the God of peace — [Who is] the Author and the Giver of peace...Strengthen (complete, perfect) and make you what you ought to be, and equip you with everything good that you may carry out His will; [while He Himself] works in you and accomplishes that which is pleasing in His sight, through Jesus Christ.

HEBREWS 13:20,21 AMP

PROMISES

For thus says the Lord God, "Behold, I Myself will search for My sheep and seek them out. As a shepherd cares for his herd in the day when he is among his scattered sheep, so I will care for My sheep and will deliver them from all the places to which they were scattered on a cloudy and gloomy day. I will feed My flock and I will lead them to rest," declares the Lord God. "I will seek the lost, bring back the scattered, bind up the broken, and strengthen the sick."

EZEKIEL 34:11,12,15,16 NASB

I will lead the blind by ways they have not known, along unfamiliar paths I will guide them; I will turn the darkness into light before them and make the rough places smooth. These are the things I will do; I will not forsake them.

ISAIAH 42:16 NIV

I will not contend for ever, neither will I be angry always, for [were it not so] the spirit [of man] would faint and be consumed before Me, and [My purpose in] creating the souls of men would be frustrated. I have seen his [willful] ways, but I will heal him; I will lead him also, and will recompense him and restore comfort to him and to those who mourn for him.

ISAIAH 57:16,18 AMP

Therefore thus says the Lord...Jacob shall not then be ashamed, not then shall his face become pale [with fear and disappointment because of his children's degeneracy].
For when he sees his children [walking in the ways of piety and virtue], the work of My

hands in his midst, they will revere My name;
they will revere the Holy One of Jacob and
reverently fear the God of Israel. Those who
err in spirit will come to understanding, and
those who murmur [discontentedly] will accept
instruction.

ISAIAH 29:22-24 AMP

Thus says the Lord, In an acceptable and
favorable time I have heard and answered you,
and in a day of salvation I have helped you;
and I will preserve you...Saying to those who
are bound, Come forth; to those who are in
spiritual darkness, Show yourselves — come
into the light.

ISAIAH 49:8,9 AMP

And you shall know — with an acquaintance
and understanding based on and grounded in
personal experience — that I am the Lord: for
they shall not be put to shame who wait for,
look for, hope for and expect Me. For thus says
the Lord, Even the captives of the mighty shall
be taken away, and the prey of the terrible shall
be delivered; for I will contend with him who
contends with you, and I will give safety to
your children and ease them.

ISAIAH 49:23,25 AMP

For though the mountains should depart and the hills be shaken or removed, yet My love and kindness shall not depart from you, nor shall My covenant of peace and completeness be removed, says the Lord, Who has compassion on you.... And all your...children shall be disciples — taught of the Lord [and obedient to His will]; and great shall be the peace and undisturbed composure of your children.

ISAIAH 54:10,13 AMP

EXAMPLE

God allows His children to make their choices:

"God wasn't at all pleased; but he let them do it their way, worship every new god that came down the pike — and live with the consequences."

ACTS 7:42 THE MESSAGE

The father of the Prodigal Son also allowed his child to learn from his own mistakes. He did not nag him or drag him back home, but prayerfully watched for his return, received him back without condemnation, and celebrated his change of heart.

"While he was still a long way off, his father saw him and felt compassion for him, and ran and embraced him and kissed him.... The father said to his slaves...'Let us eat and celebrate; for this son of mine was dead and has come to life again; he was lost and has been found.'"

LUKE 15:20,22-24 NASB

Q: I HAVE MADE A TERRIBLE MISTAKE WITH MY CHILD, AND I FEEL SO GUILTY. WHAT SHOULD I DO?

A: I'm glad...that you were jarred into turning things around. You let the distress bring you to God, not drive you from him. The result was all gain, no loss. Distress that drives us to God does that. It turns us around. It gets us back in the way of salvation. We never regret that kind of pain. But those who let distress drive them away from God are full of regrets, end up on a deathbed of regrets.

And now, isn't it wonderful all the ways in which this distress has goaded you closer to God? You're more alive, more concerned, more sensitive, more reverent, more human, more passionate, more responsible. Looked at from any angle, you've come out of this with purity of heart.

2 CORINTHIANS 7:9-11 THE MESSAGE

Just see what this godly sorrow produced in you!...You showed that you have done everything you could to make things right.

2 CORINTHIANS 7:11 NLT

INSTRUCTIONS

He who conceals his sins does not prosper, but whoever confesses and renounces them finds mercy.

PROVERBS 28:13 NIV

Blessed is he whose transgressions are forgiven, whose sins are covered. Blessed is the man whose sin the Lord does not count against him.

PSALM 32:1,2 NIV

When I kept it all inside, my bones turned to powder, my words became daylong groans. The pressure never let up; all the juices of my life dried up. Then I let it all out; I said, "I'll make a clean breast of my failures to God." Suddenly the pressure was gone — my guilt dissolved, my sin disappeared.

PSALM 32:3-5 THE MESSAGE

Confess your sins to each other and pray for

each other so that you can live together whole and healed. The prayer of a person living right with God is something powerful to be reckoned with.

JAMES 5:16 THE MESSAGE

"Go, and I, even I, will be with your mouth, and teach you what you are to say."

EXODUS 4:12 NASB

PROMISES

Is anyone crying for help? God is listening, ready to rescue you. If your heart is broken, you'll find God right there.

PSALM 34:17,18 THE MESSAGE

He heals the heartbroken and bandages their wounds.

PSALM 147:3 THE MESSAGE

For thus says the high and lofty One Who inhabits eternity, Whose name is Holy: I dwell in the high and holy place, with him also who is of a thoroughly penitent and humble spirit, to revive the spirit of the humble, and to revive the heart of the thoroughly penitent — bruised with sorrow for sin.

ISAIAH 57:15 AMP

If we walk in the Light as He Himself is in the Light, we have fellowship with one another, and the blood of Jesus His Son cleanses us from all sin. If we say that we have no sin, we are deceiving ourselves, and the truth is not in us. If we confess our sins, He is faithful and righteous to forgive us our sins and to cleanse us from all unrighteousness.

1 JOHN 1:7-9 NASB

He will turn the hearts of the fathers to their children, and the hearts of the children to their fathers.

MALACHI 4:6 NIV

PRAYERS

Create in me a pure heart, O God, and renew a steadfast spirit within me.

PSALM 51:10 NIV

Have mercy on me, O God, according to your unfailing love; according to your great compassion blot out my transgressions. Wash away all my iniquity and cleanse me from my sin. For I know my transgressions, and my sin is always before me.

PSALM 51:1-3 NIV

Now may our Lord Jesus Christ Himself, and our God and Father, who has loved us and given us everlasting consolation and good hope by grace, comfort your hearts and establish you in every good word and work. The Lord is faithful, who will establish you and guard you from the evil one.

2 THESSALONIANS 2:16,17; 3:3 NKJV

EXAMPLE

Forgiveness and restoration require a change of heart and actions. Joseph tested his older brothers to make sure they had changed (Genesis 44:18–34) before he revealed himself to them and restored fellowship with them:

Then his brothers came and bowed low before him. "We are your slaves," they said.

But Joseph told them, "Don't be afraid of me. Am I God, to judge and punish you? As far as I am concerned, God turned into good what they meant for evil. He brought me to the high position I have today so I could save the lives of many people".... And he spoke very kindly to them, reassuring them.

GENESIS 50:18-21 NLT

Q: MY HUSBAND AND I
ARE HAVING SOME PROBLEMS.
WHAT CAN WE DO TO
IMPROVE OUR MARRIAGE?

A: Be agreeable, be sympathetic, be loving, be compassionate, be humble. That goes for all of you, no exceptions. No retaliation. No sharp-tongued sarcasm. Instead, bless — that's your job, to bless. You'll be a blessing and also get a blessing.

1 PETER 3:8 THE MESSAGE

Say only what is good and helpful to those you are talking to, and what will give them a blessing.

EPHESIANS 4:29 TLB

Share each other's troubles and problems.

GALATIANS 6:2 TLB

INSTRUCTIONS

"Here is a simple, rule-of-thumb guide for

behavior: Ask yourself what you want people to do for you, then grab the initiative and do it for them."

Matthew 7:12 the message

When you do things, do not let selfishness or pride be your guide. Instead, be humble and give more honor to others than to yourselves. Do not be interested only in your own life, but be interested in the lives of others.

Philippians 2:3 ncv

Get rid of all bitterness, rage and anger, brawling and slander, along with every form of malice. Be kind and compassionate to one another, forgiving each other, just as in Christ God forgave you. Be imitators of God, therefore, as dearly loved children and live a life of love.

Ephesians 4:31-5:2 niv

Out of respect for Christ, be courteously reverent to one another.

Wives, understand and support your husbands in ways that show your support for Christ. The husband provides leadership to his wife the way Christ does to his church, not by domineering but by cherishing. So just as the church submits to Christ as he exercises such leadership, wives should likewise submit to their husbands.

Husbands, go all out in your love for your wives, exactly as Christ did for the church — a love marked by giving, not getting. Christ's love makes the church whole. His words evoke her beauty. Everything he does and says is designed to bring the best out of her, dressing her in dazzling white silk, radiant with holiness. And that is how husbands ought to love their wives. They're really doing themselves a favor — since they're already "one" in marriage.

EPHESIANS 5:21-28 THE MESSAGE

Honor Christ by submitting to each other.

EPHESIANS 5:21 TLB

Wives, yield to the authority of your husbands, because this is the right thing to do in the Lord. Husbands, love your wives and be gentle with them.

COLOSSIANS 3:18,19 NCV

Be good wives to your husbands, responsive to their needs. There are husbands who, indifferent as they are to any words about God, will be captivated by your life of holy beauty. What matters is not your outer appearance — the styling of your hair, the jewelry you wear, the cut of your clothes — but your inner disposition. Cultivate inner beauty, the gentle, gracious kind that God delights in.

The same goes for you husbands: Be good husbands to your wives. Honor them, delight in them. As women they lack some of your advantages. But in the new life of God's grace, you're equals. Treat your wives, then, as equals so your prayers don't run aground.

1 PETER 3:1-4,7 THE MESSAGE

"Don't pick on people, jump on their failures, criticize their faults — unless, of course, you want the same treatment. That critical spirit has a way of boomeranging. It's easy to see a smudge on your neighbor's face and be oblivious to the ugly sneer on your own. Do you have the nerve to say, 'Let me wash your face for you,' when your own face is distorted by contempt?...Wipe that ugly sneer off your own face, and you might be fit to offer a washcloth to your neighbor." MATTHEW 7:1-5 THE MESSAGE

"Be easy on people; you'll find life a lot easier.
Give away your life; you'll find life given back,
but not merely given back — given back with
bonus and blessing. Giving, not getting, is the
way. Generosity begets generosity."

LUKE 6:37,38 THE MESSAGE

"If you give, you will get! Your gift will return
to you in full and overflowing measure, pressed
down, shaken together to make room for more,
and running over. Whatever measure you use
to give — large or small — will be used to
measure what is given back to you."

LUKE 6:38 TLB

For the whole law can be summed up in this
one command: "Love your neighbor as yourself." But if instead of showing love among
yourselves you are always biting and devouring
one another, watch out! Beware of destroying
one another.

GALATIANS 5:14,15 NLT

It is obvious what kind of life develops out of
trying to get your own way all the time: repeti-
tive, loveless, cheap sex; a stinking accumulation
of mental and emotional garbage; frenzied and

joyless grabs for happiness; trinket gods; magic-show religion; paranoid loneliness; cutthroat competition; all-consuming-yet-never-satisfied wants; a brutal temper; an impotence to love or be loved; divided homes and divided lives; small-minded and lopsided pursuits; the vicious habit of depersonalizing everyone into a rival; uncontrolled and uncontrollable addictions; ugly parodies of community. I could go on.

This isn't the first time I have warned you, you know. If you use your freedom this way, you will not inherit God's kingdom.

GALATIANS 5:19-21 THE MESSAGE

Where do you think all these appalling wars and quarrels come from? Do you think they just happen? Think again. They come about because you want your own way, and fight for it deep inside yourselves. You lust for what you don't have and are willing to kill to get it. You want what isn't yours and will risk violence to get your hands on it. You wouldn't think of just asking God for it, would you? And why not? Because you know you'd be asking for what you have no right to. You're spoiled children, each wanting your own way.

JAMES 4:1-3 THE MESSAGE

"In your anger do not sin": Do not let the sun go down while you are still angry, and do not give the devil a foothold.

EPHESIANS 4:26,27 NIV

A man's discretion makes him slow to anger, And it is his glory to overlook a transgression.

PROVERBS 19:11 NASB

Keeping away from strife is an honor for a man, but any fool will quarrel.... A plan in the heart of a man is like deep water, but a man of understanding draws it out.

PROVERBS 20:3,5 NASB

Make this your common practice: Confess your sins to each other and pray for each other so that you can live together whole and healed. The prayer of a person living right with God is something powerful to be reckoned with.

JAMES 5:16 THE MESSAGE

Let the peace of Christ keep you in tune with each other, in step with each other. None of this going off and doing your own thing. And cultivate thankfulness.

COLOSSIANS 3:15 THE MESSAGE

If ye have bitter envying and strife in your hearts, glory not, and lie not against the truth. This wisdom descendeth not from above, but is earthly, sensual, devilish. For where envying and strife is, there is confusion and every evil work.

JAMES 3:14-16 KJV

Do the hard work of getting along with each other, treating each other with dignity and honor.

JAMES 3:18 THE MESSAGE

Those who are peacemakers will plant seeds of peace and reap a harvest of goodness.

JAMES 3:18 NLT

PROMISES

Lord, you establish peace for us; all that we have accomplished you have done for us.

ISAIAH 26:12 NIV

For he himself is our peace, who has made the two one and has destroyed the barrier, the dividing wall of hostility.

EPHESIANS 2:14 NIV

I can do all things through Christ who strengthens me.

PHILIPPIANS 4:13 NKJV

[Not in your own strength] for it is God Who is all the while effectually at work in you — energizing and creating in you the power and desire — both to will and to work for His good pleasure and satisfaction and delight.

PHILIPPIANS 2:13 AMP

God can do anything, you know — far more than you could ever imagine or guess or request in your wildest dreams! He does it not by pushing us around but by working within us, his Spirit deeply and gently within us.

EPHESIANS 3:20 THE MESSAGE

"If you want a happy life and good days, keep your tongue from speaking evil, and keep your lips from telling lies. Turn away from evil and do good. Work hard at living in peace with others. The eyes of the Lord watch over those who do right, and his ears are open to their prayers. But the Lord turns his face against those who do evil."

1 PETER 3:10-12 NLT

No temptation has overtaken you except such as is common to man; but God is faithful, who will not allow you to be tempted beyond what you are able, but with the temptation will also make the way of escape, that you may be able to bear it.

1 CORINTHIANS 10:13 NKJV

The Lord knows how to rescue godly people from their trials.

2 PETER 2:9 NLT

PRAYERS

We pray that you'll have the strength to stick it out over the long haul — not the grim strength of gritting your teeth but the glory-strength God gives. It is strength that endures the unendurable and spills over into joy.

COLOSSIANS 1:11 THE MESSAGE

Now the God of peace...Make you perfect in every good work to do his will, working in you that which is wellpleasing in his sight, through Jesus Christ.

HEBREWS 13:20,21 KJV

With this in mind, we constantly pray for you...that by his power he may fulfil every

good purpose of yours and every act prompted
by your faith.

2 THESSALONIANS 1:11 NIV

We pray for you all the time — pray that our
God will make you fit for what he's called you
to be, pray that he'll fill your good ideas and
acts of faith with his own energy so that it all
amounts to something. If your life honors the
name of Jesus, he will honor you. Grace is
behind and through all of this, our God giving
himself freely, the Master, Jesus Christ, giving
himself freely.

2 THESSALONIANS 1:11,12 THE MESSAGE

EXAMPLE

*David and Bathsheba's relationship got off to a
bad start: adultery, deception, even murder. Yet,
with God's forgiveness, grace, and help, they over-
came their problems, and God used their union to
bless all the nations of the earth:*

A record of the genealogy of Jesus Christ the
son of David, the son of Abraham: Abraham
was the father of Isaac, Isaac the father of
Jacob, Jacob the father of Judah and his broth-

ers...Jesse the father of King David. David was the father of Solomon, whose mother had been Uriah's wife.

MATTHEW 1:1,2,6 NIV

Solomon tells how David and Bathsheba worked together to teach him God's wisdom:

When I was a boy in my father's house, still tender, and an only child of my mother, he taught me and said, "Lay hold of my words with all your heart; keep my commands and you will live."

PROVERBS 4:3,4 NIV

Listen, my child, to what your father teaches you. Don't neglect your mother's teaching. What you learn from them will crown you with grace and clothe you with honor.

PROVERBS 1:8,9 NLT

Q: I AM TOTALLY OVERWHELMED
BY MY RESPONSIBILITIES.
HOW CAN I COPE WITH
ALL THIS STRESS?

A: "Do not let your hearts be troubled. Trust in God; trust also in me.... Peace I leave with you; my peace I give you. I do not give to you as the world gives. Do not let your hearts be troubled and do not be afraid."

JOHN 14:1,27 NIV

Don't fret or worry. Instead of worrying, pray. Let petitions and praises shape your worries into prayers, letting God know your concerns. Before you know it, a sense of God's wholeness, everything coming together for good, will come and settle you down. It's wonderful what happens when Christ displaces worry at the center of your life.

PHILIPPIANS 4:6-8 THE MESSAGE

INSTRUCTIONS

Pile your troubles on God's shoulders — he'll carry your load, he'll help you out.

PSALM 55:22 THE MESSAGE

"Come to me. Get away with me and you'll recover your life. I'll show you how to take a real rest. Walk with me and work with me — watch how I do it. Learn the unforced rhythms of grace. I won't lay anything heavy or ill-fitting on you. Keep company with me and you'll learn to live freely and lightly."

MATTHEW 11:28-30 THE MESSAGE

"What I'm trying to do here is to get you to relax, to not be so preoccupied with getting, so you can respond to God's giving. People who don't know God and the way he works fuss over these things, but you know both God and how he works. Steep your life in God-reality, God-initiative, God-provisions. Don't worry about missing out. You'll find all your everyday human concerns will be met.

"Give your entire attention to what God is doing right now, and don't get worked up

about what may or may not happen tomorrow.
God will help you deal with whatever hard
things come up when the time comes."

MATTHEW 6:31-34 THE MESSAGE

"Here's what I want you to do: Find a quiet,
secluded place so you won't be tempted to role-
play before God. Just be there as simply and
honestly as you can manage. The focus will
shift from you to God, and you will begin to
sense his grace."

MATTHEW 6:6 THE MESSAGE

"This is the resting place, let the weary rest";
and, "This is the place of repose."

ISAIAH 28:12 NIV

PRAYERS

The minute I said, "I'm slipping, I'm falling,"
your love, God, took hold and held me fast.
When I was upset and beside myself, you
calmed me down and cheered me up.

PSALM 94:18,19 THE MESSAGE

You are my hiding place! You protect me from
trouble, and you put songs in my heart because
you have saved me.

PSALM 32:7 CEV

Teach me wisdom.

PSALM 51:6 ICB

We also pray that you will be strengthened with his glorious power so that you will have all the patience and endurance you need. May you be filled with joy, always thanking the Father.

COLOSSIANS 1:11,12 NLT

PROMISES

"I have told you these things, so that in me you may have peace. In this world you will have trouble. But take heart! I have overcome the world."

JOHN 16:33 NIV

I love you, O Lord, my strength. The Lord is my rock, my fortress and my deliverer; my God is my rock, in whom I take refuge. He is my shield and the horn of my salvation, my stronghold.

PSALM 18:1,2 NIV

A thousand may fall at your side, ten thousand at your right hand, but it will not come near you.... If you make the Most High your dwelling — even the Lord, who is my refuge — then no harm will befall you, no disaster will come near your tent.

PSALM 91:7,9,10 NIV

No temptation has seized you except what is common to man. And God is faithful; he will not let you be tempted beyond what you can bear. But when you are tempted, he will also provide a way out so that you can stand up under it.

1 CORINTHIANS 10:13 NIV

How blessed the man you train, God, the woman you instruct in your Word, providing a circle of quiet within the clamor of evil.

PSALM 94:12,13 THE MESSAGE

When anxiety was great within me, your consolation brought joy to my soul.

PSALM 94:19 NIV

But those who hope in the Lord will renew their strength. They will soar on wings like eagles; they will run and not grow weary, they will walk and not be faint.

ISAIAH 40:31 NIV

Because the Sovereign Lord helps me, I will not be disgraced.

ISAIAH 50:7 NIV

I can do all things through Christ who strengthens me.

PHILIPPIANS 4:13 NKJV

If you need wisdom — if you want to know what God wants you to do — ask him, and he will gladly tell you.

JAMES 1:5 NLT

Wisdom and truth will enter the very center of your being, filling your life with joy.

PROVERBS 2:10 TLB

EXAMPLE

When Moses was overwhelmed with the responsibility of caring for the nation of Israel, God provided wisdom and a plan that took the pressure off:

"What you are doing is not good. You and these people who come to you will only wear yourselves out. The work is too heavy for you; you cannot handle it alone. But select capable men from all the people...and appoint them as officials over thousands, hundreds, fifties and tens. That will make your load lighter, because they will share it with you."

EXODUS 18:17,18,21,22 NIV

Q: I BELIEVE IN GOD AND I GO
TO CHURCH. IS THAT ENOUGH...
OR IS THERE MORE?

A: He...said, Men, what is it necessary for
me to do that I may be saved?

And they answered, Believe in and on the
Lord Jesus Christ — that is, give yourself up to
Him, take yourself out of your own keeping
and entrust yourself into His keeping, and you
will be saved.

ACTS 16:30,31 AMP

Jesus replied, "I assure you, unless you are born
again, you can never see the Kingdom of God."

"What do you mean?" exclaimed Nicodemus.
"How can an old man go back into his mother's womb and be born again?"
Jesus replied, "The truth is, no one can enter
the Kingdom of God without being born of
water and the Spirit. Humans can reproduce
only human life, but the Holy Spirit gives new
life from heaven."

JOHN 3:3-6 NLT

For God so greatly loved and dearly prized the world that He [even] gave up His only-begotten (unique) Son, so that whoever believes in (trusts, clings to, relies on) Him shall not perish — come to destruction, be lost — but have eternal (everlasting) life.

JOHN 3:16 AMP

Anyone who trusts in him is acquitted; anyone who refuses to trust him has long since been under the death sentence without knowing it. And why? Because of that person's failure to believe in the one-of-a-kind Son of God when introduced to him.

JOHN 3:18 THE MESSAGE

And all who trust him — God's Son — to save them have eternal life.

JOHN 3:36 TLB

For if you do not believe that I am He [Who I claim to be] — if you do not adhere to, trust in and rely on Me — you will die in your sins.

JOHN 8:24 AMP

Q: JESUS, I WANT TO BELIEVE IN
YOU. HOW CAN I BE SURE YOU
ARE REALLY REAL?

A: You will seek Me, inquire for and require
Me [as a vital necessity] and find Me; when
you search for Me with all your heart, I will be
found by you, says the Lord.

JEREMIAH 29:13,14 AMP

"For everyone who asks receives, and he who
seeks finds, and to him who knocks it will be
opened."

MATTHEW 7:8 NASB

All who seek the Lord will praise him. Their
hearts will rejoice with everlasting joy.

PSALM 22:26 NLT

The person who has My commands and keeps
them is the one who [really] loves Me, and
whoever [really] loves Me will be loved by My

Father. And I [too] will love him and will show (reveal, manifest) Myself to him — I will let Myself be clearly seen by him and make Myself real to him.

JOHN 14:21 AMP

INSTRUCTIONS

Before you trust, you have to listen. But unless Christ's Word is preached, there's nothing to listen to.

ROMANS 10:17 THE MESSAGE

For what I received I passed on to you as of first importance: that Christ died for our sins according to the Scriptures, that he was buried, that he was raised on the third day according to the Scriptures, and that he appeared to Peter, and then to the Twelve. After that, he appeared to more than five hundred of the brothers at the same time

1 CORINTHIANS 15:3-6 NIV

To these He also presented Himself alive after His suffering, by many convincing proofs, appearing to them over a period of forty days and speaking of the things concerning the kingdom of God.

ACTS 1:3 NASB

There are also many other things that Jesus did, which if they were written one by one, I suppose that even the world itself could not contain the books that would be written.

JOHN 21:25 NKJV

These have been written so that you may believe that Jesus is the Christ, the Son of God; and that believing you may have life in His name.

JOHN 20:31 NASB

For you know that God paid a ransom to save you from the empty life you inherited from your ancestors. And the ransom he paid was not mere gold or silver. He paid for you with the precious lifeblood of Christ, the sinless, spotless Lamb of God. God chose him for this purpose long before the world began, but now in these final days, he was sent to the earth for all to see. And he did this for you.

Through Christ you have come to trust in God. And because God raised Christ from the dead and gave him great glory, your faith and hope can be placed confidently in God.

For you have been born again. Your new life did not come from your earthly parents because the life they gave you will end in death. But this new life will last forever because it comes from the eternal, living word of God.

1 PETER 1:18-21,23 NLT

Can you imagine the breathtaking recovery life makes, sovereign life, in those who grasp with both hands this wildly extravagant life-gift, this grand setting-everything-right, that the one man Jesus Christ provides? Here it is in a nutshell: Just as one person [Adam] did it wrong and got us in all this trouble with sin and death, another person did it right and got us out of it. But more than just getting us out of trouble, he got us into life!

ROMANS 5:17,18 THE MESSAGE

PROMISES

He is real and...he rewards those who truly want to find him.

HEBREWS 11:6 NCV

"No one's ever seen or heard anything like this, never so much as imagined anything quite like it — what God has arranged for those who love him." But you've seen and heard it because God by his Spirit has brought it all out into the open before you.

We didn't learn this by reading books or going to school; we learned it from God, who taught us person-to-person through Jesus, and we're passing it on to you in the same first-hand, personal way.

The unspiritual self, just as it is by nature, can't receive the gifts of God's Spirit. There's no capacity for them. They seem like so much silliness. Spirit can be known only by spirit — God's Spirit and our spirits in open communion.

1 CORINTHIANS 2:9,13-15 THE MESSAGE

God once said, "Let the light shine out of the darkness!" This is the same God who made his light shine in our hearts by letting us know the glory of God that is in the face of Christ.

2 CORINTHIANS 4:6 NCV

PRAYERS

I pray for you constantly, asking God, the glorious Father of our Lord Jesus Christ, to give you wisdom to see clearly and really understand who Christ is and all that he has done for you. I pray that your hearts will be flooded with light so that you can see something of the future he has called you to share.... I pray that you will begin to understand how incredibly great his power is to help those who believe him.

EPHESIANS 1:17-19 TLB

Hear my voice when I call, O Lord; be merciful to me and answer me. My heart says of you, "Seek his face!" Your face, Lord, I will seek.

PSALM 27:7,8 NIV

EXAMPLE

"Doubting Thomas" said he had to see for himself that Jesus was alive (John 20:24,25). Jesus appeared to him and said:

"Put your finger here; see my hands. Reach out your hand and put it into my side. Stop doubting and believe." Thomas said to him, "My Lord and my God!"

JOHN 20:27,28 NIV

Jesus said, "So, you believe because you've seen with your own eyes. Even better blessings are in store for those who believe without seeing."

JOHN 20:29 THE MESSAGE

Q: IS THERE SOMETHING
I NEED TO DO TO BEGIN
A RELATIONSHIP WITH
YOU, LORD? HOW DO
I GET STARTED?

A: Salvation that comes from trusting
Christ...is already within easy reach. In fact,
the Scriptures say, "The message is close at
hand; it is on your lips and in your heart."
For if you confess with your mouth that Jesus
is Lord and believe in your heart that God
raised him from the dead, you will be saved.
For it is by believing in your heart that you are
made right with God, and it is by confessing
with your mouth that you are saved. As the
Scriptures tell us, "Anyone who believes in him
will not be disappointed."

ROMANS 10:8-11 NLT

"The word that saves is right here, as near as
the tongue in your mouth, as close as the
heart in your chest." It's the word of faith that

welcomes God to go to work and set things right for us.

ROMANS 10:8 THE MESSAGE

PROMISES

To all who believed him and accepted him, he gave the right to become children of God. They are reborn! This is not a physical birth resulting from human passion or plan — this rebirth comes from God.

JOHN 1:12,13 NLT

Therefore, if anyone is in Christ, he is a new creation; old things have passed away; behold, all things have become new.

2 CORINTHIANS 5:17 NKJV

God our Savior showed us how good and kind he is. He saved us because of his mercy, and not because of any good things that we have done. God washed us by the power of the Holy Spirit. He gave us new birth and a fresh beginning. God sent Jesus Christ our Savior to give us his Spirit. Jesus treated us much better than we deserve. He made us acceptable to God and gave us the hope of eternal life.

TITUS 3:4-7 CEV

If we say we have fellowship with God, but we continue living in darkness, we are liars and do not follow the truth. But if we live in the light, as God is in the light, we can share fellowship with each other. Then the blood of Jesus, God's Son, cleanses us from every sin.

If we say we have no sin, we are fooling ourselves, and the truth is not in us. But if we confess our sins, he will forgive our sins, because we can trust God to do what is right. He will cleanse us from all the wrongs we have done.

1 JOHN 1:6-9 NCV

PRAYERS

Say the welcoming word to God — "Jesus is my Master" — embracing, body and soul, God's work of doing in us what he did in raising Jesus from the dead. That's it. You're not "doing" anything; you're simply calling out to God, trusting him to do it for you. That's salvation. With your whole being you embrace God setting things right, and then you say it, right out loud: "God has set everything right between him and me!"

ROMANS 10:9,10 THE MESSAGE

Q: I know about God the Father and have received Jesus as my Savior. What's the Holy Spirit's role in my life?

A: I will give you a new heart and put a new spirit in you; I will remove from you your heart of stone and give you a heart of flesh. And I will put my Spirit in you and move you to follow my decrees and be careful to keep my laws.

EZEKIEL 36:26,27 NIV

INSTRUCTIONS

He washed away our sins and gave us a new life through the Holy Spirit. He generously poured out the Spirit upon us because of what Jesus Christ our Savior did.

TITUS 3:5,6 NLT

The name of our Lord Jesus Christ and the power of God's Spirit have washed you and made you holy and acceptable to God.

1 CORINTHIANS 6:11 CEV

The power of the life-giving Spirit has freed you through Christ Jesus from the power of sin that leads to death.

ROMANS 8:2 NLT

When I think of the wisdom and scope of God's plan, I fall to my knees and pray to the Father, the Creator of everything in heaven and on earth. I pray that from his glorious, unlimited resources he will give you mighty inner strength through his Holy Spirit.

EPHESIANS 3:14-16 NLT

You should behave...like God's very own children, adopted into his family — calling him "Father, dear Father." For his Holy Spirit speaks to us deep in our hearts and tells us that we are God's children. And since we are his children, we will share his treasures — for everything God gives to his Son, Christ, is ours, too.

ROMANS 8:15-17 NLT

When the Holy Spirit controls our lives, he will produce this kind of fruit in us: love, joy, peace, patience, kindness, goodness, faithfulness, gentleness, and self-control.

GALATIANS 5:22,23 NLT

The Friend, the Holy Spirit whom the Father will send at my request, will make everything plain to you. He will remind you of all the things I have told you.

JOHN 14:26 THE MESSAGE

Jesus said to his disciples: If you love me, you will do as I command. Then I will ask the Father to send you the Holy Spirit who will help you and always be with you. The Spirit will show you what is true. The people of this world cannot accept the Spirit, because they don't see or know him. But you know the Spirit, who is with you and will keep on living in you.

JOHN 14:15-17 CEV

The Spirit shows what is true and will come and guide you into the full truth. The Spirit doesn't speak on his own. He will tell you only what he has heard from me, and he will let you know what is going to happen.

JOHN 16:13 CEV

When the Comforter (Counselor, Helper, Advocate, Intercessor, Strengthener) comes

Whom I will send to you from the Father, the
Spirit of Truth Who comes (proceeds) from the
Father, He [Himself] will testify regarding Me.

JOHN 15:26 AMP

As it is written in the Scriptures: "No one has
ever seen this, and no one has ever heard about
it. No one has ever imagined what God has
prepared for those who love him." But God
has shown us these things through the Spirit.

The Spirit searches out all things, even the
deep secrets of God. Who knows the thoughts
that another person has? Only a person's spirit
that lives within him knows his thoughts. It is
the same with God. No one knows the
thoughts of God except the Spirit of God.
Now we did not receive the spirit of the world,
but we received the Spirit that is from God so
that we can know all that God has given us.

1 CORINTHIANS 2:9-12 NCV

Those who trust God's action in them find
that God's Spirit is in them — living and
breathing God!

ROMANS 8:5 THE MESSAGE

The Holy Spirit helps us in our distress. For
we don't even know what we should pray for,

nor how we should pray. But the Holy Spirit prays for us with groanings that cannot be expressed in words. And the Father who knows all hearts knows what the Spirit is saying, for the Spirit pleads for us believers in harmony with God's own will.

ROMANS 8:26,27 NLT

Dear friends, use your most holy faith to build yourselves up, praying in the Holy Spirit.

JUDE 20 NCV

Pray in the Spirit at all times with all kinds of prayers, asking for everything you need.

EPHESIANS 6:18 NCV

On the final and climactic day of the Feast, Jesus took his stand. He cried out, "If anyone thirsts, let him come to me and drink. Rivers of living water will brim and spill out of the depths of anyone who believes in me this way, just as the Scripture says." (He said this in regard to the Spirit, whom those who believed in him were about to receive. The Spirit had not yet been given because Jesus had not yet been glorified.)

JOHN 7:37-39 THE MESSAGE

He gave them this command: "Do not leave

Jerusalem, but wait for the gift my Father promised, which you have heard me speak about. For John baptized with water, but in a few days you will be baptized with the Holy Spirit."

ACTS 1:4,5 NIV

"You will receive power when the Holy Spirit comes on you; and you will be my witnesses in Jerusalem, and in all Judea and Samaria, and to the ends of the earth."

ACTS 1:8 NIV

And everyone present was filled with the Holy Spirit and began speaking in languages they didn't know, for the Holy Spirit gave them this ability.

ACTS 2:4 TLB

Then Peter stepped forward with the eleven other apostles and shouted to the crowd... "What you see this morning was predicted centuries ago by the prophet Joel:

'In the last days, God said, I will pour out my Spirit upon all people. Your sons and your daughters will prophesy, your young men will see visions, and your old men will dream dreams. In those days I will pour out my Spirit upon all my servants, men and women alike,